Contents

Editorial

So as we know, Yes did not prevail. This editorial team sat in the offices of Freight Books on the night of the Referendum, watching count after count declare No after No, and faced the reality that most of our compatriots remain unconvinced about the merits of a Scottish State independent from Westminster's control.

The arguments over fear-versus-hope and whether Yes lost or No won have been regularly reheated and served up over the past four months and we don't intend to revisit them here; although Harry Giles has one view in his polemic on p75 and his poem on p164. What has become clear, however, is that the run-up to 18th September and the vote itself were something remarkable: an entire populace politically awakened, a young generation galvanised, and a turnout unheard of in recent electoral history. Of that, we can be very proud. It was a level of engagement that those of us in the cultural sector can only dream of, but like much contemporary communication often it was conducted in the echo chamber of social media – and herein lies a parallel with certain self-absorbed literary movements. As we said when we founded this mag, the Internet at its worst is a cacophony. At its best it is a powerful weapon for change, but during the referendum campaign the Yes side over-relied on it – failing to reach beyond its social media beachhead to engage with print- and static website-using older voters, who voted no in droves.

September was the end of the beginning. The demographic breakdown of the Yes vote was overwhelmingly under 50 years of age, and while this means that time is on our side (sorry, Mum & Dad...) it does not absolve us from reaching out to the Baby Boomer generation who raised us and to continue to make the case for change. This is where the arts come in: if the 1997 devolution referendum took some of the sting out of our activism, 2014 should reactivate it and remind us how, after 1979 we in the arts "had generally been assigned the task of keeping Scottishness and the idea of the Scottish nation alive"[1]. It is time for a third Scottish Renaissance. For our part, we will continue to advocate for a strong literary culture and to encourage new voices and new directions in print.

This editorial team are digital migrants, rather than natives. That is to say, by accident of birth we occupy the unique timeframe that saw a permanent, world-changing revolution in information and communications technology. We remember a time of Banda duplicators, black-and-white photocopiers, Tippex, faxes, daisy-wheels, and dot-matrix. We remember the invention of QuarkXPress and Photoshop. We remember message-boards, internal memos, call-boxes, phonecards or running out of change. We remember hand-searching journal indexes and microfilm. And we're not even that old (combined age 110 years).

We know this gives us a different perspective on cultural linearity from those two decades younger than us, and that this difference is perhaps more marked than at any time in recent history. It is like the world before and after Gutenberg.

We have no idea what will happen to publishing, politics, music and literature in twenty, even ten years once the digital natives have taken over and we are quietly awaiting Altzheimer's. Perhaps, given the persistence of vinyl and the over-exaggerated death of the printed book (as we have said elsewhere, ye cannae wrap an eBook...), things will look much the same, and on the surface, they probably will (where are our Hoverboards now?), but there is a great danger in the rise of non-linearity.

While we would never be so naïve as to insist on the existence of a single objective truth (most EU-based media would have us believe there is nary a Nazi salute or daubed swastika to be seen on the streets of Kiev or Odessa...), last year's developments in Ukraine suggest that we are entering a new, frightening, non-linear world. This was nowhere more evident than in the Russian government's use of traditional and social media to create an uncertain portrayal of reality that exceeds even the best fictions of the NKVD and the KGB. To watch Russian state TV these days is to watch hubris that would make Stalin or Goebbels proud.

We console ourselves that it could never happen here, but it already has – beginning with New Labour spin in the late 1990s and continuing through the Better Together 'Vow', to the ridiculous, evidence-free conspiracy theories that populate the comments pages of even the most respected websites. There is no chief propagandist, we have no need for one: we have been so spun, that we are now spinning ourselves. There is a real danger that unlimited access to information without context, evidence, self-awareness and intellectual rigour may do us real, lasting, social and political damage.

It is with sadness that we bid farewell this issue to our Managing Editor Helen Sedgwick, who has been with *Gutter* since the very start. Helen was the first person we asked to join the team after the initial Begg-Searle head-to-head that began the adventure. It is testament to her hard work and dedication first as Reviews Editor and subsequently also as Managing Editor that we are still here seven years later. Helen has left to focus on her own writing and her work as Managing Director at Cargo Publishing and we wish her every success. We will miss her proofreading nous and her eye for unsolicited submissions, many new writers have appeared in these pages thanks to Helen's advocacy for their work.

In Helen's place, we are very pleased to welcome Henry Bell as Managing Editor and we offer our sincere thanks to Kate Tough and Richard Strachan for their work as standby Reviews Editors over the last six months. Henry is the editor of several books of poetry and prose, most recently *A Bird Is Not a Stone*, translations of Palestinian poets by Scottish writers.

This issue has a remarkable lack of writing about the referendum result (but then, our deadline was less than six weeks later). In its stead, we have strong new prose from, among others, William Letford, Olga Wojtas and Lesley Glaister – which we are very proud to include in an issue that contains new work from two of our most eminent writers, Janice

Galloway and Alasdair Gray, both making their first appearance in the magazine. Welcome.

As ever, it was hard to whittle down the poetry from the large block of quality submissions received. We are pleased to have *Gutter*-debut work from Dorothy Lawrenson, Roddy Shippen, and Tariq al-Karmy (whose poetry also features in the aforementioned *A Bird is Not a Stone*). And we are glad that Cheryl Follon, last heard from in her 2010 Bloodaxe collection, *Dirty Looks*, has decided to end that long silence here with eight poems from a new sequence called 'Silly Billies'.

As we write this, our thoughts are very much with our surviving French comrades-at-pens at a fellow small plucky magazine in Paris, and with all those who grieve for lost loved ones. We do not want to exist in a world where thugs with Kalashnikovs and grenades want to mow down elderly cartoonists and execute young Muslim police officers in cold blood, nor a world where Jewish people are shot while doing their groceries.

The late Stephane Charbonnier said of *Charlie Hebdo* that, "The animating intention behind the magazine's work was to satirise and provoke in a distinctive voice, one that would not sit easily in other publications." Sound slightly familiar? We may not always succeed, but the raison d'être of this here wee magazine is to surprise, to challenge norms and give voice to unheard discourse. Several writers have aimed their nibs at the hegemonies of Christianity, Judaism and Islam in past issues of *Gutter*, so what happened in Paris is too close for comfort. We are only glad that prose is a subtler medium than the (to our eyes) often frankly racist stylings of Parisian *œuvres satiriques* – which to many French are honest to a plain-speaking satirical tradition.

Obviously there is a great need to mark these deaths, to argue the positives of a secular cultural life and to defend the thin black line of free expression. But there is a much greater need to resist the easy narrative of a 'clash of civilisations' and to appreciate the nuances of co-existence with other cultures: viz, work in these pages by Rached Khalifa, Defne Çizakça, Tareq al-Karmy, Nabin Kumar Chhetri, Rizwan Akhtar and Rachelle Atalla. Beware the quick fix. Informal self-censorship through fear is already alive and well in this country; we must strongly resist the 'simple plans' of those political and religious interests that would seek to formally limit our hard-gained freedoms – be they religious extremists, fascists of left or right, racist reactionary politicians (step forward, UKIP) or neo-liberal aggrandisers. These are people who fear truth, despise satire, dismiss fiction – but who thankfully inspire poetry and polemic in equal measure.

1. Morace, Robert: 'Scotland's Generation X', in *Generation X Goes Global: Mapping a Youth Culture in Motion*, Henseler, Christine (Ed.) Routledge, London, 2012.

Sometimes the island and its surprises made anything seem possible.

Almost 1948
Janice Galloway

Almost 1948

Janice Galloway

Eric Blair, also known as George Orwell, lived on the Scottish West Coast Island of Jura after his widow, Eileen, died. There, between 1946 and 1948 he wrote his last novel at Barnhill, a cottage farmhouse he shared with his rather confrontational sister, chopping wood, drawing his own water, walking miles for the doctor and using a motorbike and a dangerously small boat for travel. Occasional visits from his small adopted son were relief from this round. He returned to England to see to the publication of 1984, and died shortly after, without seeing the book's impact. It has been in print ever since. A book about organised government's surveillance and brainwashing of its own people, 1984 resonates in a fresh way to contemporary people, as does the slogan, BIG BROTHER IS WATCHING YOU.

It had been pouring all day and the gulls were laughing. He could see them wheeling over the rocks. Wet to the bone, the neck of his oilskin streaming, he settled the motorbike against the roughcast wall of the stores. Someone, he knew, would be watching from inside. Here's Mr Blair with his toothbrush moustache all set to drip over the dry goods. He is cadaverously thin. Not that they ever said such things out loud, but he knew all the same. His nose started to run. A quick check found no handkerchief, not even a pocket. Only a rip, a thin line of waxed thread where the seam had been. His sister had promised to mend it and hadn't bothered. Good old Avril, dependable in a crisis. He sniffed hard, hoped for the best, and went inside. Nothing yet, Mr Blair, the big shop woman said. She was wrapping a ration of butter for a customer, a skinny sort who tilted her eyes sideways at him from under a hat. Sometimes things take a wee while.

Oh dear. Hat lady looked over sympathetically.

Can't be helped, he said. He cleared his throat, tried a smile.

I'll have Davie bring the parcel up to Barnhill, when it comes, the shop woman said. Her arms were braced on the counter now, in charge. You'll catch your death coming and going.

I'm sturdier than I look, he said, hoping for lightness, but the women exchanged a glance. Mr Blair was not well. He should not be out in this weather. They had the look of his sister, the pair of them, all motherly contempt. Most women, except the younger sort, did. I'll try in a few days, he said. Thanks all the same.

Davie was a good enough chap, but he didn't want anyone else poking through his mail. A pistol was not a usual kind of delivery and it would cause comment. He felt conspicuous enough already on the island. Since there was gin, he took one bottle and didn't ask for lemons even as a joke. Rationing this long after the war was not, had never been, funny.

Your sister's cold is better, I hope, the big one said, ringing up. And the wee boy – Richard, is it? Both women sighed. That was a nasty fall, eh?

Richard's fine, thank you, he said, irked. Not even the doctor was discreet here.

Glass, though, and stitches, the skinny one said. They're so vulnerable at that age. No idea of danger.

No, he said.

The bell rang behind him in the middle of their best wishes. One of them waved.

At least the rain had stopped. The sea was flat as shark skin now, cloud lifting over the scatter of islets in the harbour. Deer lowing in the distance said the threat had not gone completely, however. Out here, it never did. His calves ached with cold from the drenching of drive down, every new twist on the track throwing up mud. Avril would pull faces when he got back, say he should never have gone out in the first place, but to hell with it. He had been out all day up a ladder with the apple trees only yesterday, then spent the evening on the hill, shooting rabbits. And he had made Richard carry them, blood dripping from their eyes and noses. Someone had to toughen the boy up. It mattered he should not be sentimental, given the way things might turn. The fate of the weak was to fall. Soon, they'd patch the barn roof and clear the garden ready for coming snow and sort out the rats in the loft. There was enough to do to keep both of them too exhausted to dwell. He had no intention of stopping the necessary physical labor of being in this place, or of laying what his sister called *being a Boy Scout* to rest. That was all the doctors told him – rest. Rest was not an appropriate response to encroaching lack of breath, lack of power. They had no idea what they were asking.

A shift overhead made the rain on the panniers shimmer before the light dulled again, showing the rust. All over the frame like fungus. He had carried a scythe on his back at one time, even when he drove, and it had scored the bodywork so badly the tank looked fit to split in two. It was twenty-three miles to Barnhill. If the damn thing broke down again – well, it just better not. It took three short kicks to turn over. Revving high, startling a sheep on the grass verge with the engine's sudden roar, he started the long ride back.

Past Knockrome, the road widened out into lines of rolling heather, peat and boggy turf. At the crest of the hill, the sea reappeared with its scatter of islands. Clumps of reed broke through the middle of the road, breaking what tarmac remained into a double stream. He could drive only by keeping close to the ditch, under assault by puddles and potholes, cottage loaves of dung. Today, it was slippery with leaves into the bargain, but light showed in glimpses under the heavy cloud, and it seemed he might yet manage home before another downpour. By comparison to the journey down, this was relaxation. Rest. The doctor's word, every doctor's word, wherever he turned. *Rest.*

The last time he'd had to suffer it was at Mrs Nelson's, the day of Richard's accident.

No one knew how it had happened, but the screams brought them running to find a broken chair, shattered glass and Richard, bleeding. And he'd carried him all the way from Barnhill to Mrs Nelson's, mile after sodden mile because she had the telephone, the boy bloody as a fox.

A cut to the forehead always bleeds heavy, Mrs Nelson had said. It'll not be as bad as it looks.

And soon enough the doctor had struggled up from Craighouse with his black bag and beetled into the bathroom to start stitching. Mrs Nelson had assisted, instructing Mr Blair wait outside like an expectant father. He heard muffled moans and sobs then out she had come with Richard in her arms, five puckery black lines on his brow like a name gouged into wood. The child's eyes were wet, but he had put his arms out to be taken and fallen asleep almost immediately against the familiar scent of his father's tweeds.

The doctor was in no hurry to converse. To keep things that way, Eric offered him a cigarette.

You've been out sailing, the doctor said, nodding. A wee bird told me.
I keep myself busy. Eric lit a match, not sure where things were leading. You do, the doctor said. Keep mind in a place like this, word travels. He looked down on the seated man like Zeus from Olympus, big built, bearded, determined.

Mr Blair, I feel I have to speak. I know how severe your condition is. Even if I hadn't heard, I can see for myself.

Eric stiffened. The boy didn't budge.

TB isn't impressed by pluck, the doctor said. You don't fight an illness by fighting it: it gives not a hoot about your stiocism. You can't teach it a lesson. I'm telling you this very earnestly, Mr Blair. Rest. You've a book to finish. Your publisher must be anxious even if you're not. They'd tell you the same as me, I'm sure. Rest.

And Eric had nodded, silently incensed as the doctor handed over a tube of antiseptic cream, already half-used. His nails were too clean for an islander. Suspiciously clean.

The boy will be right as rain, he said. It's you that worries me. Mrs Nelson couldn't meet his eye.

He had worked off his rage by digging peats the following day, and taken Richard along for the exercise. They had spied on plovers from the bushes then chased each other the last half-mile home. Illness was one thing: being an invalid was another. Looking back, he was sure the doctor meant well, but he was narrow. They all were. If things went on the way they were going, the war over but things unlearned, Europe would be blown to smithereens before they knew it. The bomb had changed everything. He, at least, knew it: others were turning a blind eye. If the worst happened, he could hold on in a place like this, a place too remote to pay off as a target. Here, in more senses than one, they were un-get-at-able. Doctor's advice and a so-called routine procedure had finished his wife off before her time and left father and son high and dry. Eileen. There one minute, then nothing. Nothing. Doctor's advice my arse. Whatever happened now, he had to hang on till Richard was thirteen or his sister would get hold of the boy and that would be that. Not even meaning to, just out of habit, out of a need to feel her own misery was soothed by passing it on to others. One decade. Even five – half a decade, if he got his head down. That was all he asked. In fact, he didn't ask. He'd ruddy well achieve it by means of will alone.

By Tarbert, the dark of the forest turned to sudden brightness. Across the bay, the sky lifted as he watched from purple to lavender to palest blue. If the road had not been so pitted, he would have pulled in the clutch and freewheeled to the foot of the incline. It was glorious, this freshness after the misery of so much rain, the sea wide and flat and calm. Sometimes, the island and its surprises made anything seem possible. Maybe – the thought occurred as the sun came out, searing his eyes momentarily – maybe he should find another wife. He was ill, granted, but not unreliable. A man of principle. If he finished the book, and if it sold in anything like the numbers his publisher had his fingers crossed for, he might even – what a thought! – be rich. Avril wouldn't like the idea one bit, but these days Avril didn't like anything at all. He pictured Avril, his own sister, nodding agreement while the specialist pronounced him as good as dead (*Mr Orwell, you may have less than two years at this rate*); Avril insisting he use the pen-name to get better treatment (*Let's face it, Eric, nobody will care unless they know you're the Famous George Orwell. It's the only sure asset you've got*). His hands went stiff, picturing, hearing her voice in his head. Well, whoever the world and his ruddy sister took him for, he wasn't giving up the ghost yet. He would finish the book, make some money, at least get the farm running. Now he thought of it, he'd write another will into the bargain. And another ruddy book, if he had time. Avril would send Richard to some dreadful boarding school, even after she knew what had happened there. *He needs more discipline, just the way you did. They should have been tougher.* The bitch would do it out of spite. The motorbike was bouncing over shale now, shaking him down to his bones. She wasn't getting Richard. One way or another, he'd make damned sure. It wasn't impossible to find a wife who'd sort things out afterwards the way he wanted. The way he insisted. After the war, it was easy to find women who'd marry first chance they got.

The wind was in his eyes.

Eric never wept, not even for Eileen, but from time to time, his eyes watered. He rubbed them with his left cuff as the bike scudded on. Great walls of layered rock were rising on either side obscuring the fields. Then, as he began the climb out of the valley, a crack rang out, a sound like the sky opening. At the same moment, the bike slid sharply sideways, the engine revving wildly as he rolled his grip on the handlebars. He was aware of the ditch to his left, the solid rock veering far too close, the crack of gunfire again, again as something fluttered overhead. The machine cobbled as he struggled to regain control, lost. It was then, as the bike tipped past the point of stability, he saw a face. Long and greyish, watching from the bracken, its eyes steady. The engine cut sharply as the machine crashed down onto the heather, Eric drawing back by instinctive sleight. Barely upright, he focussed on the bracken, then wheeled, checking afresh, the sound of his own heart dinning in his ears. Now, however, with the light shifted and his gaze still, he saw the face was nothing. Mere rock, a bare patch showing pale against the terra-cotta ferns. Maybe there had been no face at all, just fear. Surprise. A trick of the light. He keeled forward, breathed deep and coughed till he almost retched. Not a face, he told himself, choking. No assassin, no accuser. It was no one at all.

Miraculously, the gin was unbroken, the bike in no worse shape than before. No one, so far as he was aware, had seen his fall but the pheasants.

And they were stupid. Stupid birds with no survival instinct. Even so, people shot them. It seemed poor sport. Another burst of gunfire sounded; distant wings, flailing. He wiped his mouth. The cloth of his trousers near the knee was torn, the flesh beneath seeping slightly. Other than that, he was unscathed. He allowed his shoulders to drop, almost smiled. He was still here. He was, after a fashion, fine.

The bike started first boot. Ahead was the way to Ardlussa. Tonight, he thought, staring ahead, he'd take Richard out and they'd hunt rats in the barn with hammers. A hammer trained a neat mind, an accurate eye, at least till the parcel arrived. Things would be better when the Luger came. Meanwhile, they'd manage.

Ravens wheeled in a nearby field, cawing. He had his book to finish, the farm to attend to, his son to raise. There were, in the real world, no alternatives. He lifted his feet and descended, roaring, into the home stretch.

Bryndzové Halušky

Kathrine Sowerby

The lake had been frozen for months
and the sun stretched our five shadows
over ankle-deep snow, fresh and slashed
by cross-country skis, to the church bells
on the island that used to be the summit
of villages flooded and trapped under ice.

They assure me it will hold our weight
after plates piled with potato dumplings
and bacon fat washed down with milk,
lumpy and sour, served in wooden cups
with our scene carved into their handles
by shepherds who came here before us.

Borrowed Light

Kathrine Sowerby

The chapel sinks into the scalped hazel hillside,
its ragged diamond panes rock their wings,
bouncing pastel light into my day: dots and dashes
spell *save me* from desert winds, frosted dawns,
bone china snowfall. Paint me kitchen gold
or deep sung cream on plaster set somewhere
between smoked trout, caught salmon and cinder rose.
Keep out those trespassers in trench coats
who point and laugh, skim stones down on Mort Lake.
Who drag dead hares through my cotton fields
strung up on beatnik blue. Who take photographs
and share me like their faded pewter trophies.
I stand at the kissing gate, my coat's silver lining
tilted towards the morning sun, and spell *I will try*

An Invocation to St Fiacre
Patron Saint of Haemorrhoid Sufferers

Andy Jackson

The neighbour warned of piles, frightened
me with tales of kids outside their houses
sat too long on cold stone. I kept an icon
of your beaming likeness down my trousers;

my prescriptions piling up, unclaimed,
the word *placebo* ten years from my lips.
Whatever ails me now, there is a saint,
to autoclave my sins, absolve all leaps

of doubt. Your warm hands and bedside
manner, smiling at my ultrasonographs,
all perfection. I built a shrine to you; steroids,
popped from blister packs, shaped into a cross.

I set it by the toilet bowl, ready to believe
in anything; reiki, homeopathy, testimonials
of patients left for dead, or truths revealed
by numbers in some randomised controlled trial.

I am unsure to whom to offer this petition,
caught as I am between the tablet and the Host,
knowing that whoever pens the prescription,
it is dangerous to exceed the stated dose.

The Catechism of St. John of Capistrano
Patron saint of jurors

Andy Jackson

Divert yourself
for two weeks
(excepting the Sabbath and its eve).
Forsake the sterile supermarket,
the *mise-en-scène*
of open-plan office,
the torpor of production line;
they exist without you.

Divest yourself
of empathy, that bag of bricks.
Turn down the heating in your heart.
Redact your prayers
with their promises of love,
clemency, deliverance.
The facts, ma'am,
just the facts.

Direct yourself
to the look in an eye,
the language of concealment,
the subtle sellouts of manner.
Observe as prosecutors
rearrange denials into damnations,
transmute honesty into culpability.
It is their calling.

(cont'd)

Disinterest yourself
in consequences.
Whatever the verdict,
most of you will share
the sentence;
community service,
restitution, incarceration,
occasional acquittals.

Disengage yourself
then go back home.
Do not lie in wait for loved ones
to give themselves away,
defences to collapse.
Do not look for motive, means,
opportunity; they will always
be there, beyond reasonable doubt.

A makar's retiral

Hamish Scott

A want ti retire for ti rise at daw
an enjoy the day or the nicht sall faa
wi ma wuts thair lane that A fin the day
no a thocht ava dae A want ti hae
nor ti think on wirds that wad speak the thocht
nor ti warsle wi baith till a poem's wrocht
but the morn-cum-neer A'll evite ti clark
for thochts an thair wirds is the makar's wark
fae the day o birth ti the day o daith
fae the first o aynds ti the hinmaist braith
for ma myn at rest an ma vyce stane-dum,
ma retiral waits on ma en day cum

Bowel Screening Test

Graham Fulton

I'm over 50
and I'm ready
to test my bowel

I pull a book from the bookshelf
I don't look at the title
I put it in the toilet bowl
and cover it with luxury toilet roll

I do half a keech, stop, slap a little lump
into the space provided

close the tab, write the date,
complete the keech, dispose of the stick

The book is
A Disaffection by James Kelman

There are diagrams on the instruction leaflet
but none of them shows a book being used

This is my own invention
It has to be the correct size to fit neatly
into the bowl, create a secure platform
It needs to feel right

The second sample is
Treasure Island by Robert Louis Stevenson,
the third sample is
Lolita by Vladimir Nabokov

(cont'd)

It's totally random
I do it by touch
It has to be hardback to take the strain

I wash my hands

There is no hidden meaning

All I do now is wait

Flying

Graham Fulton

a young daytime drunk
at the back of the bus is singing
Life's a piece uv shit
                          but ah kin deal wi it
to a not-quite-as-drunk young daytime drunk
at the back of the bus
who says in retaliation
It's no
Life's a piece uv shit
                          but ah kin deal wi it –

it's
Life's a piece uv shit
                          when yi look at it –
                          fur fuck's sake
git it right!

but he goes on singing it
the wrong way anyway

Flatpack Poem

James McGonigal

Poems like IKEA diagrams
are wordless. Sounds are
their not-quite-raw materials –
pre-processed, stained
and ready to assemble –

but no-one can foresee
the finished article
stand upright or bear weight.
And so we take
its diagram by the hand

and follow step by step.
Checking drilled holes
for their precise positioning
each to each is crucial.
Ignorant of technical terms

for pegs and thingmejigs
that fix lines together we
bend like children on the floor
making a game
from bits and pieces.

How's it coming along?
It's difficult with a partner
to sidestep arguments on what
the diagram says do next.
Look. There. Idiot.

Keep going. When there are
no parts left over in the box,
the poem is complete. Now
lift it into position. OK.
Sit on it if you want.

Company

Hamish Whyte

In my dream I'm visiting Edwin Morgan
in his yellow room in the care home:
chair-bound, a shawl over his shoulders,
he's being entertained by two cats who seem
to live under the sideboard –
one of them runs through his hands
like water – it slips to the floor
in a flurry of tabby fur.

He wrote about many cats –
the French Persians having a ball,
Chinese, Russian, even Scotch cheetikiepussies
like Glaswegian Tiny who opted out
of a milk-drinking contest –
it's no surprise the pleasure he takes
in their company.

He never had a cat, or any other pet,
but his poem 'Making a Poem'
makes one, as he made all the others
to scratch and spark on pages still.

Central

Hamish Whyte

the lines
the train into
the farthest platform
the beginning to hurry
the passengers into
the crowd looking at
the clock buying
the paper squeezing into
the day
the streets
the work from
the station transformer

The Street is an Extended Phenotype

Samuel Tongue

                                    the street is an extended phenotype
          a toilet sits unplumbed   like a ceramic sousaphone
          and a yellowed condom   or dry mermaid's purse
        is DNA expressing itself   beyond the fingertips
            in torn umbrellas   hands painted around
          discarded wings   with spray cans
          ragged colours   like coloured gloves
snagged on the wire

Railings

Brian Johnstone

Scarce a wall outside a pre-war house
does not betray the past in some way

with these lines of sores, lead long ago
poured in to set what's left just rows

of stumps, still clear near to a century
since amputation proved to be the fate

of railings everywhere. No matter
that the iron languished year on year

in depots, dumps and stores. Its time
would come as surely as necessity

will always find its place. In this case
ballast in the holds of empire, rusting

right away, and come the white heat
of the revolution, science-led, all said

would forge a new land – bottoming
for ring roads, leading nowhere fast.

Poetry Reading in the Highlands

JM Henderson

Speak – Slow. Put on your Poetry Voice.
Sing! Out! Those! Words!
   like a Gaelic vocalist:
        vowel agus vowel agus vowel
don't runallyourwordstogetherlikeabeginner
Put on your serious face
and listen.
        Nodding helps too.
And don't forget to finish by explaining
the profound effect the natural world
has had on your deeper understanding of life.
Oh yes.

Dress for the occasion: something long and flowing and smock-like
yes to bangles, lots of colour in your clothes
and do something big with your hair.

Build yourself up before you go on
prepare your audience by talking to them with as much pretension as possible
refer to where you used to live
– and how you've now downsized your life to the Highlands,
       where you're much happier,
and can help and educate the locals.
Casually refer to your regular meditation sessions
and make clear your superiority as a Literary Person

And, finally, smile now and show you got the joke.
When I finish, come ask me where I'm from.
And be sure to say, 'Jolly good. Well done.'
when I say I'm local.

The Nou

Hamish Scott

The byganes haes its birns
The future haes its fykes
Sae bide i the nou
that can dae as it likes

Boys

Diana Hendry

Wherever my grandson is –
just now on holiday with us –
boys materialise, appear
as if there's some telepathic
message line which boys,
and only boys between six
and ten – are wired into.

Here they are on the doorstep,
all leggy and unintelligible,
come to claim their own.
Ours slots in, easy as the one
missing piece of jigsaw.

Off they go up the road,
shouldering, nudging, punching
each other in a kind of excess
of delight. Wherever they're going
it's impossible for us to follow.

Who had given him those scars? Or had he made them himself? I thought about my butchered bowels and what was left of them

Spine
Rachelle Atalla

Spine

Rachelle Atalla

Simon had insisted we pay for extra legroom on the flight, so we did. He also wanted the window seat, leaving me wedged in between him and an old French lady. I felt a sense of responsibility, sitting at an emergency exit, wondering if I'd have to take charge if an emergency were to happen. These thoughts were not something new. I'd often considered what it would be like in the terrible moments before a plane crash. I'd watched programmes about people inflating their life jackets before getting out of the plane and drowning because they'd floated to the top of the cabin, unable to move.

As they lowered the cabin lights the French lady turned towards me, looking for conversation. Simon was sound asleep, leaning his head against my shoulder and I begrudged him this. I wasn't brilliant with new people. Simon would have been better chatting to her.

'I have family in Salvador,' she said. Her English was near perfect. 'I try to visit at least once a year.' She clasped her hands together. They were dignified hands: wrinkled and soft, with clean nails and a delicate gold band loosely hanging around her wedding finger. 'It is a difficult journey. From Rio I wait two hours for my flight to Salvador.'

'Yes, it is a long journey,' I said, struggling for words.

She stared at me. 'Why Brazil, for you?' she asked.

'My mum was Brazilian. I had to come.'

'Do you visit often?'

'I've never been to Brazil before.' I paused. 'My mum didn't leave her family on good terms.' I hesitated. 'My dad wasn't Brazilian.'

The lady considered my response. 'But now you feel the time is right?'

'For coming to Brazil?' I asked, knowing that's what she meant. 'I've been ill.' I could feel a lump in my throat and swallowed it back. 'I'm better now, but for a while I didn't think I'd get the chance to visit.'

She acknowledged my discomfort, trying to change tack. 'Portuguese is a difficult language. Did your mother teach it to you?'

'Only basic words. She told me I was never interested learning as a child.'

The lady smiled at me, placing her hand over mine. 'You should not have brought your engagement ring. Your wedding ring, okay, but not the diamond ring.'

'We have a safe in our room,' I said.

'Okay,' she replied. 'Be careful.'

We landed at night, ordering a taxi from the tourist information desk but we couldn't understand anything our driver said. I had a small Portuguese phrasebook in my bag but it, along with my few basic words, offered us little help. I kept saying marido, husband, wanting for some reason, the taxi driver to know we were married. 'Quanto custa?' I said, asking the price, and the driver tapped on his meter.

Suddenly we saw Christ the Redeemer illuminated high up on the mountain and I grabbed Simon's arm. 'Look, look,' I said. 'Christ the Redeemer.'

Our driver glanced over his shoulder and smiled. 'Christ?' he said.

'Sim, sim, Christ,' I repeated, noticing the rosary beads hanging from his rear view mirror. I found myself relieved by our small common ground.

*

The hotel had arranged a day-tour with an English-speaking guide. Despite my need to visit Brazil, I knew very little of my mother's past. We had no family to visit; no pilgrimage to make. We visited Christ the Redeemer but it was not at all what I imagined it to be. There were queues and hoards of people trying to take photos. Everyone was smiling, excited by what towered above, but it all seemed strange to me. I stood in the shade, watching other tourists raise their arms out, mimicking Christ's stance. It wasn't special. But was anything really special, I thought, when you saw it in the flesh?

Our coach drove down the mountain, stopping occasionally on the narrow stretches of road to let other vehicles pass. I looked over at Simon who was busy inspecting the photos he'd taken. We'd barely spoken since arriving.

'No one is sure how many favelas there are in the city of Rio de Janeiro. At least four hundred...' the guide said. 'We will be passing through one shortly but do not worry. We have all doors locked.' I glanced up, trying to read the guide's expression. 'They do not pay for electricity,' he continued, 'they steal it. There is much crime here. Police cannot enter some favelas.'

As we drove through, I noticed there was a salon offering a discount on manicures and a shed that doubled as an electronics shop. Wide screen televisions sat out on the pavement and I wondered why no one had stolen them. Houses toppled over one another, steps going off in all directions, washing lines strung up on top of unfinished shacks.

'Simon, are you looking?' I asked, annoyed that his camera demanded so much attention.

He glanced up. 'Yes, it's something else, isn't it?' he said, returning his attention to the camera.

*

Copacabana beach was two blocks from our hotel. I was glad not to be facing the sea – if there were to be some natural disaster, like a tsunami, the hotels at the front wouldn't have had a chance.

We settled in our loungers and I watched as Simon applied his sun cream. He used the highest factor, oily and thick, smearing it heavily across his body. It matted the hair on his arms and legs, making him look paler than he actually was. Soon after completing this task he decided he needed the toilet. With no public toilets in sight he headed for the sea and I stayed, protecting our belongings. I'd put a swimsuit on, under my shorts and t-shirt, but couldn't bring myself to take them off. I was paranoid people would notice the slight bulge of my ileostomy bag under the swimsuit.

The beach was busy now and Simon had to carve himself a path back from the water to our loungers. I watched him grow disorientated, steering himself in the direction of other loungers, before realising he'd gone too far. A few metres to my left, a man was letting his children bury him in sand. I watched their happy faces, running around, patting more sand in against him. A woman, their mother, I suppose, took photos but without speaking or smiling. I imagined her longing to be somewhere else and me taking her place.

In the late afternoon, with a parasol protecting him from the sun, Simon fell asleep. I looked at his face as he slept, noticing how much he had changed over the last few years. He still looked youthful; a few grey hairs and only one or two wrinkles but an unease disturbed him now. Even in his sleep I could see it. Suddenly, I had an overwhelming feeling of love for him. I wanted to be close to him again. I wanted to make him laugh.

I turned to my book but my fingers were clammy, making it difficult to read. In frustration, I threw the book down and looked out across the vast expanse of beach. I noticed a young boy approaching, carefully, through the rows of people spread out in the sun. Turning his back to me, he came to a stop in front of my lounger and sat down in the sand. He wore no t-shirt, only shorts and a baseball cap that was too big for his head. He was thin, unbearably thin; a thinness that made me feel sick. He could have only been about ten but he resembled an old man – skin and bone worn away to nothing. He gripped a backpack in his right hand that looked empty. On his wrist he wore red and yellow beads – the beads could have been made for a toddler. From my lounger, I shifted slightly, giving myself an elevated view of his movements. The boy stretched himself out, placing his backpack behind his head to create a pillow. He ran his fingers through the warm sand, clawing handfuls, letting his fingers fall flat again. He moved his body from side to side, suddenly sitting up, drawing his knees close to his chin and burying his toes under the sand. In that position, I saw the entire framework of his spine. Every bone protruded out towards me, allowing me to see how he was made. He seemed hardly a person in that moment – just an arrangement of bones. He lay back down and within minutes was sleeping soundly, his face turned away from the sun. It made me wonder what would become of my bones once I was gone. I had always disliked the idea of cremation. My parents had bought their cemetery plot when I was a child, needing to be together, one on top of the other. I'd never had their foresight.

The boy could only have been asleep for twenty or thirty minutes, but for all that time I watched over him, imagining I was protecting him from whatever harm I thought might approach. He had scars on his arms; the scars pale against his dark skin. I found myself thinking pigmentation was a strange thing. Who had given him those scars? Or had he made them himself? I thought about my butchered bowels and what was left of them. I wanted this boy to know I cared for him. We were united, this boy and I, from circumstances out of our control.

He woke, rubbing his eyes slowly, and sat up, grabbing his hollow backpack. He took a yellow football top out of the bag and pulled it over his head with the baseball cap still on. Like the cap, the shirt was also too big, drowning him. There was a price tag hanging from the back of his shirt, which didn't seem to bother him. He got to his feet, weaving through the loungers and towels, until he was away, lost to me through the crowds of people.

*

I sat on the edge of the bed, listening to Simon in the shower. He'd left the door ajar and I could hear him humming. I thought about surprising him, jumping in beside him, but I couldn't do it. We had sex in the dark now, with Simon doing his best not to touch my bag and neither of us mentioning the awkwardness after.

He came out smiling, towelling his hair. 'Are you nearly ready?' he said.

I nodded, getting to my feet. 'I want to drink tonight.'

He laughed. 'Is fun Flora coming out tonight?'

'She might...'

'I'd better take my camera.'

Beach bars lined the promenade and it was difficult to decide on one. They all seemed alike. Simon chose one that had a Samba band setting up and we took a table towards the back. We both ordered caipirinhas – strong and sugary. I knew the limes would cause me trouble but decided it was worth suffering. We ordered several rounds and I could feel myself becoming giddy, clapping to the Samba, trying to get Simon to join in. He looked at me and, for a brief moment, there was a flicker of distaste in his eyes.

'Why did you look at me like that?' I said.

'Like what?' He frowned, knowing it had started.

'Like I disgust you.'

'Flora,' he said, lowering his voice. 'Of course you don't disgust me.'

I took a sip of my drink. 'I know you're not attracted to me anymore,' I said boldly, aware my eyes were beginning to sting. 'I wouldn't blame you if you wanted to be with someone else. In fact, I think you should.'

Simon gripped my arm, hurting me a little. 'Stop feeling sorry for yourself.' He cleared his throat. 'I'm not going to pretend everything's fine but we'll...' He paused, noticing a young boy standing by our table. The boy smiled at him. 'What?' Simon said.

'Olá,' the boy said. He started speaking rapidly in Portuguese and proceeded to make a flower out of pink tissue paper, offering it to me.

'Não, não,' I said, trying to hide my watery eyes. He had red and yellow beads around his wrist and I wondered if this was my boy from the beach. I chose to decide against it.

'No,' Simon said, shaking his head.

The boy placed the paper flower in my hand.

'Don't take that,' Simon said. 'If you take it you'll have to pay for it.'

'Maybe I want it,' I said, smiling at the boy.

Simon looked from me to the boy, whose smile was even wider than before. 'You really want that?' he said.

'Yes,' I said, defiantly.

Simon exhaled and reached into his pocket. The boy held up three fingers, indicating the price. Simon placed the Reals on the table and the boy snatched them away. 'Obrigado, obrigado,' he said, excitedly. The boy continued speaking, bringing his hand up and making a clicking noise with his tongue, pointing to Simon's camera.

Simon looked straight at me. 'What is it now?'

'I think he wants to know if we'd like a picture together,' I said.

'No,' Simon said. 'No, we don't want a picture.' He turned away, leaving me to face the boy alone, shrugging apologetically.

When Simon was sure the boy had gone he looked up. 'Why did you insist on buying that?'

'I felt sorry for him.'

He was quiet for a moment. 'You can't feel sorry for everyone.' He reached over, taking my hand. 'Things happen that you can't, personally, make better.'

'We're on holiday. I don't want to fight with you here. I just want to have a nice time.'

'I don't want anyone else,' he said.

We had made a reservation for dinner but instead stayed where we were and ate bar food, ordering drink after drink. We lost track of time, unaware of our voices growing louder as we made exaggerated, excited, plans for our future without considering the realities. Simon helped me out of my seat and we left, walking hand in hand, partially supporting one another. We'd made it onto the zigzagged walkway before I noticed Simon was empty handed.

'Si, where's the camera?' I asked, slurring my words.

Simon glanced down, nearly tripping on his flip-flops. He ran, unsteadily back to the bar, returning moments later with the camera, like a satchel, over his shoulder. 'Shit!' he said, before pulling me in and kissing me, pressing himself against me. 'Home,' he shouted, slapping my bum.

'How many blocks?' I said, taking his hand.

He shrugged, smiling lazily. 'You'll know better than me.'

We stumbled across the road, incoherently debating which street to turn down. It didn't seem to matter which one we chose. There were lights and people everywhere. I was safe; I was happy. We turned down by the Copacabana Palace, marvelling at its beauty. I was guiding us, leading us behind the Palace, passing little shops and cafés I swore I recognised. They were all closed but I had no concept of time. I was starting to feel dizzy and a little sick.

I took us down a quiet street, convinced it would bring us to our hotel. We laughed, unaware of the footsteps behind us. I turned, haphazardly, noticing two young boys coming towards us. One was bigger than the other and they approached us quickly, shouting to us in words we could not understand. The smaller boy I recognised – he was the boy who had made me my paper flower. I was smiling when I realised they were pointing guns at us, ushering us down one of the narrow side streets.

Everything seemed to happen slowly. I'd lost my ability to speak or scream. Simon was still holding my hand. The bigger boy shouted to the smaller one who held his gun higher, gripping it with both hands. The bigger boy lowered his gun and circled us. He started pressing his hand into my back, pushing me forward.

'Take my money,' Simon shouted, trying to empty his pockets. This gesture startled the younger boy, who took a few steps closer, the gun shaking in his small hands.

The bigger boy was pulling at my arm, gesturing for me to get down onto my knees. He started waving his gun in my face. Simon too was on his knees with his hands behind his head. My hands were clasped together; my fingers feeling foreign without my rings.

'It's okay,' Simon said as the bigger boy took the camera from his side. 'Everything will be okay, Flora.'

The camera's flash went off behind us and I knew the boy was taking a photo of us on our knees. I stared at the little boy, wondering if he was indeed my boy from the beach with his skeleton frame.

The other boy checked my pockets but they were empty. He started to pat me down, his hand stumbling against my stoma bag. He grew excited, ushering with his hand to the little boy. He lifted up my shirt, trying to discover what it was I was hiding. He stared for a moment, confused, pressing a finger against my bag. There was frantic discussion between the boys, the bigger one inspecting it closely, before they both backed away. I imagined their words of disgust and started to sob. Tears rolled down my face and I was sure death would be better than this.

The little boy, for the first time, started shouting at the bigger boy, perhaps trying to hurry him up. Simon was reasoning with them; speaking calmly with words they did not understand. I thought of my mother as a girl in this city.

A Change is as Good as a Rest

Micaela Maftei & Laura Tansley

A delicious secret, a taut thrill that tumbled straight from between her lungs to between her legs: Jess kept a mickey in her office desk drawer and her bacon bits at the back of a cupboard in the communal kitchen. Vegetarian for seven-and-a-half years, teetotal for two, a new door was opening witnessed only by the host welcoming her in. New, new, new; everything Mark did from the kitchen to the bedroom was brand new and Jess still felt the need to hide the evidence. Too many PETA pamphlets and a household where ground corned beef was a staple meant that by the time she was twelve she'd developed the idea that true saintliness was in the mooning face of a cow, or the inane repetition of a pecking chicken. The youth worker at her family's church told her that she was bright, that she was sensitive, and that if she felt closer to Jesus by not eating meat she shouldn't persist in denying herself. He'd given her a promise and a ring on a chain to wear around her neck, neither of which were kept. But the guilt persisted: like a slick layer of spit licked on and left to dry, it tingled, insisting that she keep these new things hidden.

Mark used to be straight-edge, had a winning line of tic-tac-toe crosses tattooed inside his bottom lip when he was 15. He says now he's lapsed he'll get them altered by an artist, make them skull-and-crossbones that he'll smear with his tongue, suck with his mouth 'til they rouge, stretching their edges when he turns himself inside out to show them off. The questions about sex and meat and drugs and booze that he used to return in the negative now get replies like 'why not', 'sometimes' and 'if you're paying'.

'It all changes when you meet someone you want to eat or smell something you want to fuck,' he claimed as his knife slid through his steak, the mouthful limp with tenderness, sagging at the edges as he held it on his fork.

He flexed his fingers, making his knuckles turn white like fat. For him it was about how it made him feel: visceral, tuned.

'Oh god, it melts, it's just, melting,' Jess's veal was the most expensive thing on the menu and she felt the week's wages, each calorie she no longer counted, tasting it all in an instant, churning it around and around with her tongue.

For her it was the way it made her vibrate, and how his descriptions and articulations made her feel newly, totally present. It wasn't an act either, at least not as far as she could tell. She was *there* when he talked to her, or almost there. Like a Polaroid emerging, she was a shadowy essence, and the manifestation was forming, revealing. But recently she'd been thinking of the part of a Polaroid most people forgot – the film that peels off so the image can appear. The film slots in and each picture comes out, leaving behind a black plastic sheet. That was the imprint of everything she used to consume and crave, and the rawness of what was coming out was fragile but strengthening. It was so real to her that when he talked to her or even turned to look her way, she could hear the catch, the hiss, the sliding sound as the one-time-only shot was framed, trapped then ejected.

That night they each drank a bottle of house red, tore strips from bones like tudor lords, ordered coffee with cream then cognac, dribbling rich alcohol onto pristine, lacy tablecloths, their joints stiffening with crystals of uric acid. Stains from the wine's legs filled the creases in their lips and gave them dizzying headaches and spit-inducing acid reflux. Desires swelled, turning impressions into three dimensions. She asked for a plate of bacon for desert, only half joking, and then used the heel of the bread to erase the oily juices from the oversized white plate. She fed it to him, drawing out traces of his hot mouth on her fingers after he took the bread. Where before she would have contemplated a jog after dinner, a hot shower before bed, she now looked between his eyes, focused on that less-than-an-inch, then shifted outwards to his left eye and informed him of what she wanted from him, where, which parts, how.

Mark drove a dented old car with two windows and a door not working – bent down one side as if kicked by the steel toe-cap of a boot; she'd never asked him how it happened, it was a story from a time she was no longer interested in. In the passenger seat she lowered the chair back until it looked like the road was coming straight through the windshield, right into her jawbone. When he settled himself in the driver's seat he took his wallet out of his back pocket and put it in her lap, thick and heavy warmed, softened leather, brown like butter heating in a pan. He drove with one hand on her thigh; she shifted the gears, speeding because he knew he shouldn't, the evening oiling his decisions so that they happened smooth, and flexibly joined together.

Last week her flatmate tried to have a conversation about her messiness. She'd begun kicking her mail under the dining room table because it seemed addressed to another person, a different being. She'd sort through it later, someday. He'd been trying to trap her in the kitchen or hallway for days but she barely spoke to anyone anymore, didn't even answer the phone unless it was Mark. When he finally caught her he started asking about the noises he heard at night that kept him awake but that he couldn't locate.

'Sounds like rustling,' he said, 'then murmuring and arguing, like mewling cats fighting over meat. I can't sleep, I feel like I'm going crazy.'

She didn't care if he was wound up, he needed winding up.

'Did it maybe sound like it could have been coming from outside, in the park?'

The building surrounded a small square of green that was supposed to encourage community but instead had become a place for owners to take their pets to relieve themselves. It was proving hard to foster friendship with your neighbors while seven dogs were simultaneously shitting.

'Maybe,' he said, 'have you been hearing it too?'

'Oh no, I haven't.'

'Oh.'

'Hmm.'

'Well, if you hear anything let me know.'

'Mmm. Have you sometimes been hearing a moaning, too? Like a long, low whine? Almost like a leaking seal in a pipe?'

He frowned. 'Um, no. But we should put a sign up or something, get people to check. If it's a gas pipe it could kill the whole building.'

'Yes, let's,' and she backed into her bedroom, satisfied that nothing could stick to her, that she didn't need anything that anyone else offered these days. She didn't even acknowledge the notice in the lobby that asked residents to sign up for free carbon monoxide tester kits.

Mark was hanging on to people though, their chatter, their stuff, their stories. He liked to involve others even if they thought they weren't interested at first, liked to keep the windows open and doors unlocked. He'd invite strangers to sit with them when they were having coffee or waiting at a bar for a table to open up, or when they were in a queue, or pausing to check where they were, like last Saturday.

'Excuse me, do you know where Victoria Street is?'

'Sure, it's just two blocks over,' collar up, hands in pocket, side-parted hair cows-licking out of the front of a wool hat; for Mark he was a challenge that made him change their plans.

'Oh great, we're looking for Tratestini's Deli,' a place she'd not heard of, an idea he'd not shared, another overheard comment or notation in a paper or link clicked on the web, a chain of decisions apart from her, 'because apparently their sandwiches are incredible.'

'Oh my gosh they are,' he looked them up and down then, and the no-longer-stranger took his hands out of his pockets to gesticulate his burst of interest, 'you have to try the pastrami, they make it up with this soda bread that's got egg and gherkins through it. Amazing. I need to get over there more often.'

'I'm an omnivore, I'll try anything,' Mark said.

'What's that?'

A rat, Jess thought. An oil-blue crow. A black bear.

Mark looked him in the eyes and smiled and he was a goner, completely lost.

'Why don't you come with us? You can point out what's good,' and instead of gesturing towards the deli, Mark seemed to point to Jess.

That was all it took, an appeal to people's taste, and they'd do whatever he asked. Take another beer, or a seven-and-seven, or a whisky and coke, he'd say, there's a place nearby, and because they'd come this far with him they'd think, why not see where it all ended up. When they got sleepy he'd convince them that all they needed was some more food to soak up the booze, so they'd find a pop-up restaurant that he'd read about in *Time Out*, down an alley, in someone's flat, at the back of an old warehouse.

'So how did you two meet?' he or she or they would usually ask across the upturned crate-turned-table, the barrel, the thick glass, the granite countertop.

Jess would say, 'at the circus' or 'on set'. Mark would smile and squeeze her hand and then tell some version of the truth, like 'we reached for the same napkin at Rachel's Bar and Grill', or 'when I saw her I wanted to pull her hair up and find that place, that little hollow behind her ear. You know where I mean'.

Mostly they just wanted Mark, his effusive approval, his eyes screwed up in insistence, his mouth dropped in feigned surprise. And because they wanted Mark they layered heavy looks on Jess, looks that he worked in like dough, with a forearm across her chest or a hand on her ass when they walked through a doorway. One night he bit her, pretending he thought no one was looking, and she saw their newest hanger-on, Jeremy or Justin or something, bare his teeth, exhaling through them softly and then heel-toeing it over to the men's room. Jess liked the part when they left them all heated up and confused, on the street without a way to get home because they'd spent their money and the subway was shut, she and Mark heading back to his. Under the orange streetlights and the white disinfecting glow of take-aways, these strangers stared through the situation looking for an answer or even a suggestion. She felt their confusion in the places where her skin touched her clothes.

Depending on the vibe and the encounter they might switch names on the ride home, introducing themselves to each other as the people they'd left behind, which occasionally extended into Jess shouting out a different name through the duvet in the direction of any wakeful neighbors downstairs. But in the morning the remnants were always gone, and she woke to hot coffee, minus the milk and sugar she used to weaken it with, stale bread with square sausages, and Mark once more.

The other day she'd walked past an unfinished building and stopped short at the hand-painted sign calling out to her: ARE YOU READY TO BE WHO YOU'RE BECOMING. It was either the bad punctuation or the blood-red lettering that made her eventually realize it wasn't a construction site at all but a new clothing shop, all exposed ducts and concrete floors and cashiers with razored hair and hundred-pound white t-shirts folded on steel tables. She took two bras into the fitting room – little wooden chalets with adjustable mirrors and a bench the length of her legs – then sent Mark some pictures on her phone before slinking out of the shop, using one finger to hand back the bras still clipped perfectly to their small plastic hangers.

That night they drank cocktails in a basement and met Julian, recently moved to the city and enthralled with everything that wasn't his stifling small town. Mark touched the back of his neck when he brought over a round and Julian started sweating. Emboldened, or perhaps as a response, when Mark came back from the bathroom and pronounced it cramped and red-lit, the kind of place you'd get a blowjob from a stranger, Julian blushed and declared to the table that he'd take Jess up on that, though she hadn't offered. She told him she'd take a rain check at the precise moment Mark said 'go on then, she'll meet you there,' and slid the toilet key all the way across the wobbly wooden table.

He lost a lot of his pink-cheeked air once she shut the door behind her, and the hinge of his thumb and forefinger at the base of her ear felt hard as rock.

'I don't believe it,' he muttered after he came.

'Are you ready to be who you are becoming?' she asked him, easing the key out of his loosely gripped fist to unlock the door.

He threw a tantrum when they wouldn't take him home with them, and when he called out 'pimp' Mark punched him in the cheek, horribly spinning his head over his shoulder. They left him with his head between his knees, wet from the seat of his jeans creeping up his back as he sat on the curb. That night Mark fit his fingers into the three pale blue marks on the left side of her neck where her hair became downy; nestled there like soft, furry, fruit-bruises. She imitated his voice for Mark, sketched out his posture and movements, and fell asleep with her head lodged between his chest and his arm. In the morning the marks were green like gooseberries, and the woman who sat next to her at work prodded them with a pen to try to elicit an explanation.

'Don't tell me, you ate too much Quorn mince and fell asleep on the remote control again,' she said.

'Yeah, that's it.' Jess moved the pile of overdue work from one part of the desk to another. She felt jumpy, and the woman beside her kept hitching up her tights, pulling the loose material that wrinkled around her knee-folds up towards her swollen thighs. The sound of Lycra catching on her dry skin, a hangnail scraping over the cheap polyester of her skirt, turned Jess's stomach.

'Don't you ever worry that you'll die alone?' she said, 'Like, choking on a soy bean with no one to, you know, slap you on the back?' and she hit the back of Jess's chair with her biro.

Jess slammed one of her drawers open and shut, stood up and clicked onto her desktop. If she didn't actually shut down the computer, most people would assume she'd just stepped out for a few minutes. She downed the drink from her drawer in the ladies loos, leaning against the lip of the sink, fast enough to make herself puke, and was back in bed with a bacon sandwich by four. But the oil lingered on her fingers, she couldn't wipe away the fat on the sheets, and she sucked her fingers so far into her mouth in an attempt to clean them that she was sick again.

The bruises were getting darker, and she couldn't keep her hands off them. Touching them produced a rash that spiraled down to her chest. Pulling her hair down around them made it limp and strained, wiped the colour from it somehow. Her annual leave stretched across another week from work, but this time she didn't tell Mark. In the mornings she put on her fitted shirt, hound's-tooth skirt and the high heels that hurt, left him at the bus stop and walked towards the subway that she wouldn't catch, turned a corner and took a cab instead. But secrets were oozing out of her; the bruises were brown now like moelleux aux chocolat. Daytime telly was distracting. Cookery shows gave her tips on smoking a brisket, how to make crisp crackling, create a blushing duck breast; looking at the veins of fat running down a shank of beef made her breathless, made her heart contract 'til her vision blurred and the palm she felt on her forehead was damp like a watering mouth. She ordered in sweet and sour chicken, meat lover's pizzas, even ribs, then threw it all away and drank glass after glass of cold water. The next night she tried to tell Mark, ordered a salad and gave it her best shot.

After she'd explained, he watched her for a full minute and a half, and then finally said, 'makes sense, all relationships should be about compromise.'

Jess couldn't tell if he was being sarcastic or not until he savagely cut then thrust a faintly bleeding hunk of his filet mignon onto her plate. The fork stayed stuck in, pointing out at an angle, and she was sure she could feel the heat from his hand off the metal. The lettuce seemed to wilt, and cheery little radishes were drowning in the protein the meat leaked. When she looked up at him his eyes were hard and his mouth was poised, and she knew he wasn't going to look away first.

The Main Point of Contention in the Divorce was the Wedding Photos

Olga Wojtas

We know that people feel the urge to give wedding gifts, but we're not setting up home, are we? So we don't really need stuff. What we would like is your presence and something to remind us of the day and your being part of it. So, that's what we'd like. Bring along a photo (or something else to remind us of you) and we'll put them all up at the entrance, and then gather them to keep afterwards. (Now that's much easier than the John Lewis wedding list thingy, isn't it?) — Katie and Jack.

As is customary, Katie's name was first, but it hadn't been her idea. Neither had she invited Yvonne to the wedding, and she didn't know that Jack had.

This needs clarification. Fiction writers don't write from life: if they did, they would be life writers. But they sieve their lives for nuggets, just like the gold panners up at Helmsdale. Which fits in, by the way, with the wedding theme. Did you read about that man who spent 18 months panning for gold, dredging up enough to make an engagement ring for his fiancée and wedding rings for both of them? Some people reading this will recognise the first paragraph as a message from Jeannette and Colin, a real couple who recently married.

Colin, as it happens, is my creative writing tutor, and provided the title for the story. But Katie and Jack are not Jeannette and Colin. And Yvonne, who you will have deduced is a former girlfriend of Jack's, is entirely fictional.

Having said that, I really liked the photo idea. I gave them (Jeannette and Colin: this is still the real bit) a pic of myself wearing a T-shirt with the legend 'Unreliable Narrator'. I've never liked people relying on me.

The John Lewis wedding list thingy, we had one of those. People just ignored it. Not my side; his. We really wanted a toaster. Nobody gave us a toaster, but we got a set of really naff mugs. and who the hell gives people a porcelain statuette of foxes? (His Uncle Douglas, that's who.)

But this isn't about me. I don't do life writing. I'm not reliable enough.

Let's introduce Babi. A strange sort of name. Indian? No, she's from Milngavie. It's pronounced 'Baby,' which is what her first boyfriend called her. She adopted it as her name and changed the spelling because she loved Biba; not that she could afford their clothes. She had a cute mini-cape which looked Biba-esque but came from a much more downmarket boutique. Babi obviously isn't in the first flush of youth, but it would be impertinent to probe further. Not even Jack knows exactly how old Babi is, and he's her son. Babi has never dressed or acted her age except during the Swinging Sixties. Throughout her life, she's been full of surprises. The latest surprise is that she's delighted about Jack and Katie's wedding.

She's always been so anti-marriage. But she never liked Yvonne.

What's going to happen? Is Yvonne going to turn up at the wedding with a naked selfie? Or will she send the naked selfie direct to Jack's mobile, where Katie will later find it? Or will Katie realise that Yvonne is the one guest to have turned up without a photo, and demand to know what precisely she has given Jack to remind him of her?

'It all started with the wedding photos,' she will tell the solicitor.

Penelope, the symbol of a faithful spouse, weaving and unpicking, weaving and unpicking.

Not a non sequitur. Another thread (did you see what I did there?) incorporated for several reasons. Faithful spouses make us think of unfaithful spouses. The image of weaving is intended to reassure that the different strands of the story will all come together in a coherent whole. Or perhaps, if Penelope's in unpicking mode, they won't. And the reference to the Odyssey shows that I had the benefit of a classical education. Also the reference to non sequitur, Latin for 'it does not follow'.

On her dressing table, Babi has a photograph of herself. She thinks it's atmospheric but most people would describe it as blurred. She's half turned away from the camera, her dark ringlets cascading down from under a corduroy John Lennon cap. She reckons she still has that cap somewhere and, unlike the cheesecloth shirts, it will still fit. She briefly contemplates wearing it to the wedding, but the fascinator will go better with her peacock coat. And she's in the mood to celebrate. Goodbye, Yvonne, just as it was goodbye, Rachel, and goodbye, the one before that. Katie's a sweet little thing: she won't give any trouble. Babi doesn't know that Jack has invited Yvonne to the wedding.

We were all sitting in the pub, complaining about how we never write anything. We actually call ourselves the Non-Writing Writing Group. John says: 'Writers write. That's what they do.' He also says: 'You can edit crap, but you can't edit nothing.' We make him sit at another table. I didn't tell any of them I was writing this.

Anyway, there we were, complaining, and someone, Karen, I think, said why don't we all write down a word and incorporate them in our writing. The list we came up with was idiot, image, complete, unpleasant and think.

(Actually, the list we came up with was fritter: hysteria, memorial, author and capricious, but I couldn't get that to fit, and I didn't know if fritter was a noun or a verb. Of course, complete could be a verb or an adjective. If you're getting confused, just forget about John and Karen, since they won't feature again. Anyway, they're not characters, they're people.)

Learning Portuguese.
The owl is eating a mouse.
The boy is washing his feet.

If you break your arm, you must go to the hospital.

Eggs are full of protein.

October is the tenth month of the year.

Do you think I'm a complete idiot? I can see the unpleasant image.

I made up the sentences, but they're the sort of thing you find in language classes. I once went to Jeannette's language class – she's German, and a very good tutor. I learned to say where I was from and what my name was. I don't think I could say any of the sentences above, although I remember the German for boy, egg and ten. Latin was much worse. The soldiers were always carrying spears and the girls were always decorating the table with roses.

More people learn German than Portuguese, but I didn't want to put German in case people started making inappropriate connections. I would say again that this isn't about Colin and Jeannette, but then people will think I'm protesting too much. Honestly, it isn't. I chose Portuguese because of Elizabeth Barrett Browning's *Sonnets from the Portuguese*, written when she was being courted by Robert Browning. The title's an in-joke – he called her his little Portuguese because of her dark colouring. They had a really happy marriage.

Yvonne opens the envelope and discovers the wedding invitation from Katie and Jack. She hasn't even reached the bit about the John Lewis thingy when she's torn it into tiny fragments.

The reason Katie and Jack are not setting up home is that Jack (in his forties, but it would be ungallant to fix on an age since that would lead to speculation about how old Babi is) still lives with his mother. And Katie will be moving in with them. She has agreed to this because she thinks the flat has potential, and she reckons that what with the cigarettes and the vodka, Babi won't be around for ever.

Jack can't imagine life without Babi. Did someone say Oedipus complex? Speaking as a classical scholar, I've never been happy with that term. Oedipus didn't fancy his mother: he didn't know Jocasta was his mother. And it wasn't even his idea to marry her. It was political expediency suggested by the Thebans.

Katie's just upset that after the wedding, Jack gets a pinboard to display the photographs and the central image is the one of Babi in her John Lennon cap. Wedding photographs, says Katie, are of the bride and groom. They have some of those as well, says Jack, in an album. But the album is on a shelf, says Katie, and the pinboard with guests radiating out from Mother Babi is on the wall. Jack and Babi look at one another and roll their eyes.

I had a mate who worked on *The Sun* when Kelvin MacKenzie was editor. Kelvin would prowl round the newsroom looking over reporters' shoulders at what they were writing. He would read the intro, and then shout to the subs: 'The headline is such-and-such.' He didn't say 'such-and-such,' obviously, but Kelvin's headlines were utter genius and I'm not even going to try to imitate one. The point is that the poor bloody hacks then had to make sure their story fitted in with Kelvin's brilliant headline.

I imagine most writers write the story first and then find an appropriate title. In Colin's class, we get given the title and then have to come up with an appropriate story. But life doesn't always run as smoothly as that.

There hasn't been a divorce. We've celebrated a number of anniversaries. I've never even mentioned the photograph to him, and certainly not to a solicitor. The deal with Studio Morgan was that we could get thirty prints for the album. There were dozens of pics to choose from, and I was going through them all because he wasn't that interested. He said the album would just end up on a shelf.

It was a pic taken during the reception. He was looking at her in a way he never looked at me. In a way he never looks at me. The only blessing was that she was completely unaware of it. We're still friends but I'm glad she moved to Berwick. Her husband's lovely. They've got the sort of marriage I imagine the Brownings had. Well, somebody's got to.

Nuit Blanche

Rached Khalifa

He is Rabelaisian. A Gargantua flanked by two gigantic bottles of red wine. His bald head, a gilded dome, beams from between the two minarets. He loves his red wine, food and cigarettes. Which caused him hypertension, diabetes and obesity. He doesn't mind as long as he heads his table. He is like an Ottoman sultan surrounded by a boisterous entourage. People come and go at his table. They eat and drink and talk until dawn. Some leave early while others come late. But Gargantua is imperturbable in his chair, presiding his table.

He tells the same jokes which the guests have heard a hundred times but laugh at so heartily as if they'd never done. They laugh, talk, eat and swig. He nibbles more than eats, and one wonders how he has gained all this bulk. Maybe genetic. But he likes gargantuan sizes in everything. While the guests work on chicken drumsticks and wings, he goes for an entire turkey, golden brown and glazed. Where they are served fish steaks and heads, he has a whole fish for himself served on a silver platter and garnished with lemon slices and sprigs of parsley protruding from its mouth and gills. He likes gigantic things on his table. Maybe for aesthetic reasons. Gigantism suits his gargantuanism. Normal sizes put in relief his larger-than-life proportions. Or maybe this is his approach to life and business in general. Small business is for small businessmen, he theorises. He gathered a massive fortune from trade with entire continents. In business he wages titanic wars. He is ruthless despite his *bon enfant* face. He trades with continents not countries, corporations not companies. He negotiates with territories stretching beyond racial and geopolitical boundaries. He ships merchandise to Eurasia and America, to Africa and Oceania. His guests' joke is that he can bring peace to the world better than all heads of states put together. He laughs his head off every time he hears the joke. And the guests love to repeat it to placate him and redeem their gluttony. He smiles when he recalls how he started his fortune shipping snails, lizards and scorpions to the Far East.

The sultan also loves to be flanked by literati full of wit and spirit. They enliven his table. He did little education. To be rich didn't require advanced learning, he prematurely realized. In fact, the less the better, he insists. Business is flair and luck. Education cerebralizes and reason impedes action. His philosophy is that business has its own reason that reason does not understand. A quip he gleaned from some philosopher he couldn't remember who.

Yet the sultan needs elevated themes to adorn this table. He is like a medieval patron. In olden times he would flamboyantly throw money bags to the guests after a sumptuous dinner or encomium. He relishes the thought, but he is a modern entrepreneur. Rather postmodern. He amasses his wealth from air, land, water and cybernetics. He phones, faxes, emails, text-messages and tweets. The world is compressed in the iPhone he wields now and then to clinch a deal. The universe is held in his hand like a grain of sand. The guests wonder at his sporadic fiddling with his gadget. But they know as far as there is fiddling there is serving of food and wine. He never talks about his business. They never ask.

'Our friend decided to go home for good,' says the sultan in a low voice to the scholar sitting next to him. He's his favourite. The others are engrossed in their plates and talk.

'Really? He hasn't reached the age of retirement yet!' says the scholar sardonically. His eyes glued onto his plate.

They refer to him as 'our friend,' for he is their friend. He has known the scholar for too long. They were inseparable. They studied together from primary to university. They sat next to each other in class and prepared for exams together. This nurtured a strong bond between them. However, the scholar recalls how he used to weep all night under the cover if his grades were less excellent than his friend's. He would work harder for the next exams. He would revise in secret, cloistered in his bedroom, pretending to be unwell or tired. The scheme most often paid off.

They graduated with distinction. This earned them a scholarship to study in the Sorbonne. Their dream came true. They enrolled in comparative literature. They wore long hair, flared trousers, and integrated Parisian life in the wake of Mai '68. They would quote Camus and Sartre, Homer and Virgil to impress friends and chat up girls. They rented a two-bedroom flat in Rue de La Bruyère wherein they studied, fucked and smoked hash together.

'No, he's serious this time. He said he had enough of academia. He wants to change his life radically.'

'Do you think he can?'

'He's serious.'

'What kind of change?'

The scholar is intrigued. He stops jabbing into the grouper head with fork and knife. The head is monstrous and keeps sliding on the viscous sauce.

'He wants to convert into agriculture. He says teaching no longer excites him. He finds it boring after the reforms.'

'Agriculture?! What agriculture?'

'Organic.'

'Bollocks. It's one of his whims. He's always been impulsive. It's his flaw.'

Their relationship lost some of its intensity after that night, but he still considers him his best friend, almost a twin brother. They sometimes meet up at the sultan's table and set it ablaze with wit and spark. In truth, they don't discuss. They joust and lecture and prove. They are erudite in art, literature, history, and politics. They interweave their talk with Latin witticisms from poets and philosophers the guests have never heard of. Sometimes they invent things. The audience gawks in awe. The sultan is full of pride for much of the wit and praise is credited to his magnanimity. He's the artisan of these nocturnal causeries. The patron wants to feel he is the patron. At a click of a finger or a wink of an eye or a clear of a throat things conjure up on the table. The restaurant stays open as long as he is there. In the small hours, he leaves a handsome cheque on the table.

'You know, he's already resigned. He's adamant.'

'Irresponsible. How will he feed his family?'

Gargantua clears his throat. The glasses are immediately topped. The guests are busy eating and drinking.

'What kind of agriculture you said?'

'Organic olive oil.'

'What? He surely lost his mind. He doesn't know anything about olive growing. Plus, he is a wreck. How will he manage?'

'He's depressed. He's changed a lot since the birth of his daughter.'

'I know. Nature is sometimes cruel.'

'He says he's found faith. He is a new man.'

'No, no, I can't believe it. I told you he's impulsive. He has no principles. What happened to the atheism he once brandished with panache and pride? Where has his fascination with Bakunin, Marx, Nietzsche, and Sartre gone? Poor thing, he's crumbled like a house of cards. He has no guts for radical ideas. A mere nature's blunder hurls him into metaphysical nonsense. I pity him!'

He redeems his tirade on grounds of love for his mate.

'You know how much I care about him,' he adds.

'Yes, I know. But his faith is not the faith you are thinking about. He says it is nature. He wants to invest in it. He says he finds in it peace and growth for his soul or whatever word he uses.'

'He hasn't talked to me much of late. He must be depressed. But how will he invest in nature?'

'I am going to help him,' says the sultan in a flamboyant display of magnanimity. 'He's our friend. He needs help in this time of crisis.'

His eyes search around for approving nods. But he is disappointed for the guests don't seem to have heard him. This moment should normally be a climax in the causerie. The audience would nod, praise, and even give him a standing ovation for his gargantuan generosity. Never mind, there will be other moments.

The scholar keeps silent, digging into the grouper head. The bits of meat fished out of the crevices are tasteless tonight.

There is a long pause. The host slurps from a large glass. The scholar works on his plate and head.

'But how will you help him?' he breaks the silence.

'If he has a mystical eye, I have an entrepreneurial one. There is business in there. You know, organic olive oil is a big thing in the rich world today. I've got connections.'

Here again he looks around for a climactic moment, but the guests are absorbed in their food and talk. Never mind.

'His parents have bequeathed him huge olive groves in the village, as you know. They have been neglected for decades.'

The professor nods.

'I told him he can use the land for growing organic vegetables. Why not? He should optimize the fields. He can kill two birds with one stone. I gave him a cheque of ten grand to start with. He needs to plough the land and prune the trees.'

The scholar's Adam's apple slides up and down. The head is now a heap of bones and chewed mash. The eyes have been gouged, and the brain sucked clean off its crevice.

That night Sophie was in the mood for adventure. He spoke to her in the SU Bar, for the first time. He was a little tipsy, and so was she.

'Aurais-je l'immense plaisir de vous inviter à un verre d'absinthe mademoiselle?'

He stooped and took an imaginary hat off his head, parodying fin-de-siècle gallantry. She accepted with a smile. A good start. The conversation was a little awkward at the beginning. But as more drinks came in their tongues loosened. He learned she was studying anthropology and her research project was a Lévi-Straussian approach to indigenous cultures in the Maghreb. Perfect. The Amazighs' resistance to Islamicization is his forte. Sooner or later he will have her *crue* or *cuite*.

Sophie is gorgeous. She comes from a wealthy family, however she tries to hide it. She is a bourgeois but wants to play it rough. *C'est la mode.* The Marxists and the Feminists were knocking down the edifice of Western ethnologophalloegocentrism. Her philtrum, however, betrays her pretence. Its dimple has the fineness of a girl born with a silver spoon. He has a theory about female philtra. Rather a fixation. He thinks a woman's philtrum is the key to her class, character, and sexuality. And Sophie's is indubitable.

She lives in Créteil and wears an expensive perfume. Perfume is as revealing as a philtrum. She has the beauty of a movie star—another BB. She has fair hair, long and silky, with two fine plaits she wears like a diadem. Her complexion is just perfect, worthy of a *Marie Claire* front cover. Her eyes large and contoured with shady mascara. She has a perfect nose, small, straight and arrogantly sexy. There is something magnetic about her mouth. When she speaks her lips exude this je-ne-sais-quoi. Is it the shape of her lips or the slight diastema between her front teeth?

Her body has the delicacy of a bird or a butterfly.

'We're throwing a party tonight. Why don't you join us?' he asks, cautiously trying not to be emphatic, nor indifferent.

Bourgeois birds are like fish. They are easy to scare away. A wrong step and that's it, you are left alone. He has to tread carefully. If she accepts, she is caught and will be his tonight.

Why not forever? The question flashes in his mind. She is so beautiful, so lovable. How strange one is so quickly attached to someone he's just known. Is it love? Maybe. Perhaps most likely. This is the first time he has such feelings and thoughts.

She nods. That's it. Yeah she's coming to his party. The butterfly is caught in his web. Oh flutter and flail my fair lady of a fairy-tale!

He doesn't know exactly when he lost her. She stuck to him at the beginning of the party then vanished like an aisling behind the misty forest of drifting bodies and smoke. Everyone was stoned. Smoke floated and cast a screen you could cut with a knife. Booze ran à flots and genuine Moroccan weed languorously moved from lip to lip. Students from all races danced, drank, smoked, kissed and romped like nymphs and satyrs in the heart of the cityscape.

Late at night when smoke cleared and human density thinned out he caught them kissing on the sofa. They kissed languidly like molluscs. Their tongues were entwined, their hands buried in crotch and thigh, and their eyes tight shut.

He couldn't fall asleep that night. In the silence of the small hours he could hear their muffled grunts and groans in the adjacent room. The bed creaked and whined. He wept in silence under the cover, like when he was a schoolboy.

When they went for brunch the next day they were chatty and excited and buoyant. He dragged his feet behind them, sullen and taciturn.

'I am very upset about what happened last night,' he said out of the blue when his friend went to the loo. 'You came to the party with me, but you dumped me for another. It's not fair.'

The word 'another' startled him. He meant to mention his friend's name but it didn't come out.

She looked at him in feigned shock, and said 'And so what?'

She had that bourgeois arrogance and effortlessness when she spoke. This made her more attractive to him. Her diaphanous complexion glowed in the glorious light of the morning.

'But you came with *me*!' He screamed.

'Do you take me for a piece of furniture?' Her fine nose and philtrum twitched this time.

'But why did you go with *him*?'

Again he couldn't bring himself to mention his name. It was stuck somewhere in his throat. He couldn't tell whether it was linguistic or psychic hindrance.

She paused and then said, 'He has poetry in him.'

So curt, so hurt. His friend showed up. End of story.

'Do you think he can manage?' the scholar asks the sultan again.

'Yes, I am sure he will.'

'But the man is a shadow of himself. He is skeletal. He has lost so much weight. I suspect he has cancer. He was such a handsome guy with his long wavy hair and bold cheek bones. You would take him for a Grecian god, an Apollo. He attracted women like moths. He was so lucky.'

Almost compulsively he feels his double chin. It now hangs like a pelican's. He always knew he would have it one day.

'It's not physical. There will be other people to do the job,' says the host. 'He will be in charge of management and logistics. I have already secured him a contract in France. When the season kicks in I will give him another cheque to pay the workers and cover the overheads. In two or three years' time—*inshallah*—he will have his own oil press. There is a lot of potential in there.'

The patron is now ebullient and expansive. He raises his gargantuan glass and draws a noisy draught. He is happy with himself, with his performance.

'But people gossip in the village,' says the scholar.

'Gossip?'

'Yes, they gossip.'

'Gossip about what, whom?'

'About you.'

'They gossip about *me*?' The sultan grimaces, shrugging off the thought.

'They say you asked him not to cash the cheque before the end of the month.'

'Bollocks! Who's saying that?'

'They say he talks in the café.'

Everything but slander. The sultan's image is immaculate back home. He never balks when it comes to helping the villagers. It is his ritual to give gifts to the poor. Stationery at the beginning of school, esparto baskets filled with goodies in Ramadan, and lambs on the Sacrifice Day.

'Preposterous. It's not true. How can I ask him to do so when what I spend on this table every night is far more than what I gave him? Ridiculous!'

The patron's rosy face turns into dark red. A faint twitch rides the left corner of his mouth. He slumps into deep thought.

He has never seen him in such a dark mood.

'But you know, he's depressed. He probably has cancer. He needs *your* help.'

He snaps at the professor's words.

'Hell with him and with his cancer! Why is he spreading lies about me? Why is he ruining my reputation? This is betrayal. Yes, betrayal. He betrayed our friendship. He betrayed my trust. He was so depressed last time I saw him. I felt sorry for him. I wanted to help him. Why is he doing this to me? I tell you why—it's jealousy eating him up. What a fucking pathetic slanderer!'

The guests are in shock. They've never heard him swear or seen him lose his temper.

They stare at him obsequiously. They don't seek to understand for they fear they might infuriate him further.

He leans over the scholar and says in a low, defeated voice, 'Sorry for being rude. Thanks for opening my eyes. Your honesty is much appreciated, dear friend.'

'Don't mention it, please.'

'I will stop the cheque tomorrow morning and cancel the deal.'

A rooster crows somewhere nearby. Its shrill tears the translucent silence of the morning. Shafts of light, resolute and laser-like, surprise them through the window curtains. Fuck, it's another *nuit blanche*, smiles the professor as he stands up to leave.

The Age of Reason

David Crystal

was a horse I never backed
but *Black Dave* and *The Mongoose*
were my all weather bankers
in the Winter of 2013.
Only a beast would steal
a signed CFC football
from a Sue Ryder shop
and what kind of publican
puts up a sign demanding
a minimum spend of £6.50
on Sky TV football nights?

Asif my barber has a new offer
a PC health check and a hair cut for £8.00.
Sometimes he nicks my neck moles with his cut throat
normally during a jealous rant, against *Uncle*
who lives in Dulwich and imports Tea.
I like Earl Grey and Grey Goose vodka, grey seagulls are OK
but it takes a lot to beat the beauty of a grey wagtail
on a river bank, anywhere on a warm sunny day.

Flights

Chris Powici

one heron is a slow thrown spear

greylag rise from the pale winter grass
like shook trees

siskin are god-motes
twisting in a yellow wind

peewits are Stukas in love

skein-shapes of the pinkfoot
are longbows drawn
and longbows shot and trembling
harps, rivers, the knot in your heart unravelled
your heart's blood streaming

and billowing in the tractor's wake
gulls are spindrift
gulls are snow

Thomas Glover's Nagasaki
a journey in Japanese forms

Colin Will

haiku

In the warm Japanese air
a strong fragrance of flowers
Aberdeen gull sounds

sedoka

A man in a box
carried through the streets,
by four mud-splashed men

To each side
people prostrate themselves
in un-reflecting puddles

tanka

height of her white forehead,
black hair swept back
small cherry mouth –
no expression, but a sense
of where a smile might hide

somonka

Glover-san rough, red face
hairy man shout,
drink too much sake, laugh,
fall into bed, where I remove
coarse Scottish tweeds

(cont'd)

You have what I crave,
a sweet softness,
the delicate aroma of flowers,
a touch light as eyelashes,
your pale, tender skin

death poem

griping pain every night
pissing blood the servants see
emptying pots, saying nothing.
I was always too strong
to admit to being weak.

Navigating the *Enola Gay*
Theodore 'Dutch' Van Kirk (27 Feb 1921–28 Jul 2014)

ML Gill

Do I regret

the Susquehanna River, my first compass needle:
flat after flat of coal, the unrelenting quiet
of swift water, my father's hands at the oars?

What I did

was get us there, and back. I've always known
the way; maps a decoy, instruments
a poor pantomime of river bed, ridges of stone.

that day?

The earth tilted 159 degrees,
43 seconds to out-fly the shock.
Cyanide pills in Tibbet's pocket.

No sir,

we didn't know if the plane would shred.

I do not

navigate now. Instead, I sit and watch
children at play as long as they will allow.
I've asked to be buried facing east.

Samizdat

Brian Johnstone

Starved of the like by dictat
before their arrest, irony comes

with the library cart
making the rounds of the cells

with what they had craved
in samizdat: multiples

typed through a carbon sheet,
passed over in trams, left

on a prearranged bench out
in a park: books they had sought

up to the end of their liberty,
here now in this cell block,

in the bleakness of concrete,
by the dim of a single bulb:

the volumes marked as unfit,
safe to be read since no-one

will make it back to a past
they know has already been lost.

Damsel

Fran Baillie

Wummin, scootin aboot yon lochan
in yir smirrt silks o turquoise an cobalt,
d'yi ken jist how bonnie yi are or
d'yi ging aboot the world pynin ti be
a licht-hertit Admiral or Cubbage White?

Afore lang yi'll be dwynin awa,
Mither Nature's wye o daein,
laivin iz ahent, heelster-gowdie
in luv wi yi, aye myndin o
mi wummin in air-blue.

Miles

Chris Powici

Nineteen years after the death of my father I'm cycling through a crowd of twisted
scots pines on the Sheriffmuir Road thinking about the family trip to Romania in
1970 and dad standing in a Timisoara back yard – aunts, cousins, uncles, in-laws,
fluttering madly about a rough trestle table laden with ham, bread and homemade
lemonade, thirty years of war and exile falling away like the petals from the cherry
tree, and dad as deeply calm and happy as I've ever seen him, as if all this din of love
were the breeze from the river or the swell of birdsong and the thought happens that
if I could look at myself right now I'd see a fifty one year old man criss-crossed by pine
shadows crammed full of things to say and sing and speechless.

Pepos and False Berries

Jonathan Bay

knock on my watermelon
hollow belly
smell the top of my head
for ripeness
pluck me out
of the deep damp bed
throw me in the sun

let my juices
stain the knife
scoop seed from flesh
and flesh from seed
set them out to dry
save the black tears through winter
then return them to the soil

turn my right toward summer
turn my left to earth

Death

Nabin Kumar Chhetri

In the first week of August, we moved to a new place
leaving that house where I was born. The garden,
the kitchen, the living room and the mango tree
next to my window where each season, nothing grew.

That year, the villagers were dying one by one.
the epidemic hit every house
killing everyone almost as a God would.

I remember how my grandmother died one morning
letting out her breath in small instalments
as though she was paying her debts to the life she owed.

Later that year, strangely enough, the mango tree
filled with fruits, from green they turned pink and yellow.
All over Bhojad, the street smelt of them. At night,
the wind carried the smell to as far as Devghat.

I'm sober again, like my
wits have been knocked
into me, but my top lip
has begun to ache.

A Small Scale Disturbance
William Letford

A Small Scale Disturbance

William Letford

The barmaid's pouring the same pint but now she's looking at me with big wide eyes and everyone has parted and a space has formed around me. The floor has been tiled with slate, and there's Joe, down on the slate floor grunting and hissing and struggling with some guy that's wearing a bright blue jumper. They don't look pretty. The guy gets on top of Joe. I lean down to slide my forearms beneath his armpits so I can drag him off but my balance isn't right and I stagger as I get hold of him. Drops of blood appear on the back of his blue jumper. I snap back to full consciousness and realise that this is the guy that's just stuck the nut in me.

There's a thud at the top of my spine and my jacket is yanked back so hard I feel the zip at my collar dig into my Adam's apple. I'm still hooked onto the guy below me and whoever has a hold of my jacket is trying to lift both of us at once using my neck as leverage. I'm choking. I see Joe and he has these big wide eyes just like the barmaid and he's still hissing through his teeth and clawing upward. Someone else gets a grip of my face and there's calluses at the base of his fingers and he tries to pull me up and with him stretching my neck and the collar of my jacket slicing inward I fear my head may be sheared straight off.

I let go. The relief is instant and the room sweeps about me, ceiling, floor, pints of lager, people staring, then a big bald face, it's Lex, the bouncer, and I know this guy. He used to lift weights with my Uncle Richard and just like that it comes to me that he had a very strict fondness for Asian porn then he uses my body to barge open the door and I'm back outside.

Hyde's is a basement pub. A flight of stairs lead up into the street. He drags me up the steps but I don't struggle, I'm happy to be out of there and I'm coughing and I spit onto the pavement. I'm lying face down so I stand up to muster some dignity and the street-lights are blurred because tears have gathered in my eyes.

Big bald Lex is staring and he's standing with his shoulders back and his arms crossed in front of him. No, not staring, he's looking through me, like he doesn't know me. He has assumed this impassive posture and something about that makes me want to drive my fist an inch through his face.

The door swings open and Joe is flailing like a cat and the bouncer's having trouble forcing him up the steps. Lex turns to help his partner and Joe shouts, 'We were in there two minutes, we haven't even got our fucking jackets off.' They wrestle him up the steps and push him down onto the pavement and he springs up like he's made of rubber. He screams, 'It's that cunt in there that should be out here.' He points at me. 'Look at his fucking face.'

I get in front of him and I say, 'Joe, fuck up man.'

He grabs me by the shoulders and he's breathing hard and it's like I can see the adrenaline in his eyes and he says, 'Look at your face.' I place a hand over my nose and it comes away covered in blood. The front of my jacket is smeared with blood and there are droplets dotted over the pavement.

I say, 'You've got a bottle of whisky back at the flat.'

He says, 'Two.'

I say, 'We can start swingin and end up in a cell or we can go back to your bit and drink.'

He's still got a hold of my shoulders and he takes one deep breath and says, 'Let's go.'

Halfway along the street I expect Joe to turn round and shout and point but he doesn't, he keeps walking but he's still breathing hard and his hands are clenched into fists and it's a nice night, a bit on the cold side but it feels good to be out in the fresh air. I'm sober again, like my wits have been knocked into me, but my top lip has begun to ache. I tap my front teeth and they're numb like I've been at the dentist. I touch my nose and nothing happens. Then I pinch it and there's a spike of pain.

I stop Joe and ask if my nose is broken. He takes the examination seriously, shifting my head from side to side. A clutch of people are walking towards us. They take a wide berth when they see my face, and something about this makes me feel good.

He says my nose looks fine and we turn off the main road. There's a chip-shop ahead. Two men are outside the shop using plastic forks to stab at their chips and they're swaying like they've had a skin-full. Each time they lift a clump of chips their heads bow to meet the food. Light from inside the chippy has brightened the pavement and as we pass through the brightness one of the men says something that ends in, 'that.' 'Face on that,' or 'state eh that.' Whatever he says, Joe spins round to challenge him and I have to hold Joe back and I get in between them and I say, 'Joe, what the fuck is wrong with you?' He shrugs me off and continues walking. I turn to apologise but the guy is standing like a mute, with his plastic fork in one hand, a haggis supper in the other, and more chips crammed into his mouth than looks comfortable. I don't bother.

I catch up with Joe and he has his hands in his pockets and he says, 'That wasn't my fault in there, back at the pub, he was out for it. That guy left his house the night knowing that was going to happen.'

The blood feels cold on my skin. I use my jacket sleeve to wipe it from my face then I twist the sleeve round to find some fresh material and dab my nose to check if it's still bleeding. I say, 'Don't worry about it.'

We reach his close and his keys jangle as he opens the door. The bulbs have gone so there's no light and every stone step is worn in the centre by I don't know how many footprints. I place my hand against the wall to steady myself. We get to the first floor. Joe opens his door and shouts, 'That's us back,' and before I'm fully into the hall he asks for my jacket. His hallway is all wooden flooring except for a large square rug in the centre. I say I'm going to the toilet and he says not to drip over his rug so I hold my hand beneath my nose as I walk. Les comes out of the living room and she's smiling and she says, 'Hi Bill.' I use my free hand to wave then close the bathroom door behind me.

The tiles are white and the surfaces are clean. This makes the room seem sterile. I take a moment, then place my hands on either side of the sink and lift my head to look in the mirror. My nose is swollen but that's it. Nothing squint, no black eyes, not as much blood as I imagined. Why am I disappointed?

I run the tap, scrunch up toilet paper, soak it, and dab my face. Les raises her voice. 'That's right,' she shouts, 'Joe Crighton, two pun heavier than a bag of sugar and a mouth like a fire alarm.'

Les and Joe do this a lot, it's the way they hold back the boredom. Specks of blood have dried around my mouth. I scrape them off with my fingernails. I'm pale, and the idea of slinging whisky down my throat suddenly doesn't appeal to me.

I hear Joe raise his voice and he says, 'Have you seen Bill's face? Sometimes you can't get out of it, Les.'

Les replies, 'Can't get out of it, and what had to be done? Did Bill's face have to be thrown in front of the guy? Cause there's not a mark on you.'

I open the bathroom door and turn into the kitchen. Joe is in front of the sink. He's hand-washing my jacket. Les is standing by the kettle with three mugs lined up beside it. She seems relaxed, not wound up one bit. She winks at me as I walk in. The situation strikes me as oddly domestic. Joe is dunking my jacket in and out of soapy water, Les has the tea on the go and I've just walked out of the bathroom with a freshly washed face. I take a seat at the table and Les says. 'Bill, you're going to have to go to the hospital with that.'

Joe whips his head round to look at me.

Les starts laughing when she sees the expression on Joe's face, 'Good Saturday night then,' she says, 'down at the pub, rammie n that.'

I say, 'let the jacket soak, Joe.'

He drops the jacket into the water then slumps into a chair and leans forward with his elbows on the table.

When Les places the tea in front of us she says, 'You'll win the next one.' She lifts her tea to her mouth and I'm sure she's using the rim of the mug to hide a smile. Joe is staring down at the table and Les turns to me and rolls her eyes. She says, 'So what happened, and I'm asking you, Bill.'

Joe lifts his head to look at her, it's hard to read his expression. I say. 'We came in to the pub and went to the bar to get a drink, there were two guys sitting there, one of them was wearing a flat cap and he said, 'Go somewhere else and get served.' I took a few steps to the right. Next thing the guy's off his seat and he's facing me and he says. 'Your pal ruffled ma hat.' Les is still staring, so I add, 'And that's it, that's what happened.'

Joe says, 'He went for Bill because he wanted to take the tallest out first.'

Les says, 'Pure nonsense.'

Joe says, 'It's about dignity, Les.'

She looks at us, one after the other, 'It's got nothing to do with dignity. What you're talking about is self respect. Dignity comes from somewhere deeper,' she says, 'in fact; I think you're born with it.'

Joe looks at the table again, he says, 'Were you born with it, Les?'

Les is still for a moment, 'The question is why would you doubt that I was born with it?'

Joe shoves his chair back and seems about to say something, almost stands up, then sits back down again. I laugh, but Les doesn't, and Joe says, 'That's right Les, why would I doubt that you were born with dignity. Why would I doubt the person that shares my bed, shares my life, was born without it.' He closes his mouth, and looks away, like he's finished, then adds, 'the person that I love.' He looks back at her, 'I bumped into Marc today.'

Les lowers her head.

I pick up my tea.

Joe says, 'No denial. That'll be the dignity taking over.'

I put my tea down before it's reached my mouth. They're staring at each other. Les has an expression so flat it's almost dead. Joe's fists are clenched again. I should leave but I'm fascinated.

Joe says, 'This is it you know.'

Les nods her head gently.

Joe stands up and his fists are still clenched, he says, 'Slag.'

Les blinks.

Joe moves his arm, retracts his elbow slightly. Les clocks the movement and she's staring at his fist. Joe lets his arm fall straight. Les stands up smoothly, grabs her mug and slams the contents into Joe's face. Tea splashes everywhere, over the table, over me, over the wall. Joe's standing stock still and his eyes are squeezed shut. He brings his hands up to wipe his face and I'm wincing because I know the tea must be hot and as his hands are rising Les swings the empty mug over her shoulder and cracks it down onto the top of his skull. The mug splits at the handle, clatters across the work-surface and lands in the sink. Joe takes a couple of steps back, gets his balance but keeps moving backward then he turns and continues right out of the kitchen. There's a loud bang like he's kicked the front door then the door opens and he slams it behind him.

Les sits down and drops the handle of the mug onto the table. She looks at me, 'Out,' she says.

Which is fine, who'd want to sit here anyway?

The front door didn't close properly when Joe slammed it. I walk through and close it behind me. I hear Joe leave the close and think about following him. But that is a disaster waiting to happen. I stand in the dark and hang fire until Joe is well gone. I'm cold without my jacket.

When I get to the foot of the close and open the front door a black cab rocks up on a drop off. Best thing that's happened to me all night. Four women tumble out of the taxi. When all of their high heels have hit the pavement I jump inside.

I like black cabs, there spacious, more like being in a carriage than a car. That's what I'm telling myself anyway. I'm telling myself I'm in a black carriage and I'm leaving the rest of the night behind.

The speaker system destroys my fantasy. Crackling. Lots of it. Fucking annoying. The driver's trying to say something and I'm saying, 'What?' and the only thing I've got to go on are his eyes in the rear view mirror. Staring at me. Glancing at the road then staring at me again. The speaker system is most definitely fucked so I lean forward and put my lips to the wee gap you poke your money through.

I say, 'What?' and he says something but the crackling covers it and I've already told him where I want to go so I just say, 'Aye,' and lean back.

The streets are better from the back of a cab. The distance is good. Watching is good. We're rolling towards the high street and we hit some traffic. There's a restaurant to my right and some smokers are gathered outside. One pair of long legs lead to a short skirt and three men are hovering. The woman opens her purse and drops a set of keys. When the keys hit the ground I hear the sound, the jangle, like it's inside the cab. Like she's dropped them inside the cab right beside me. She bends to pick them up and the men turn in formation.

The lights change and the taxi rolls on and I'm wondering about the sound and the driver's eyes look at me again through the mirror. Blue eyes. We turn a corner and two men with their arms around each other throw their heads back and laugh and the laughter is with me in the cab. The speakers are picking up the sound from outside. Amplifying it. Surely no. Is that even possible?

The word, 'cunt' enters the cab, then, 'love, I love it!' and on and on and sentences come and go like street-lights and it's loud. I put my lips to the hole again, where money passes from the passenger to the driver. I say, 'There's something wrong with your speakers. They've been turned inside out.' He just gives me his blue eyes. I lean back. Fuck this. You know what I want? I want it to snow, and when the snowflakes hit the ground I want them to be as big as kisses.

Seconds later, she let rip with a wail of blood-chilling intensity, of almost heartbreaking anguish. Catastrophe! I thought. She's impaled herself on the swivel chair!

Soggy Bottom Baby
Ian Macpherson

Soggy Bottom Baby

Ian Macpherson

The queue in the chemist's wasn't happy. The assistant wasn't happy. And I was about to get furious. At this stage, however, I was in complete control.

'The word escapes me at present,' I said, 'but it's related to women and it's got 'men' in it.'

'Menstruation?' suggested the assistant.

'Not menstruation.'

'Hymen?'

'Nope.'

'Women?'

'Not women.'

'How about mental?' muttered the man behind me impatiently. 'That's got men in it.'

'Not' – and I was getting a bit testy at this stage – 'mental.'

Just then the manageress came over. 'What seems to be the trouble?' she enquired. Several people gave their versions, I gave mine.

'Menopause,' she said.

'That's the one. Right. Now here's the problem in embryo. I bought these condom 12-packs, buy 2 get one free. So far, so excellent. I'd just begun to open the wrapper on *this*, the free packet, prior to – well, let's not go into that. There are ladies present. Anyway, no sooner had I begun than the one true love of my life said 'Whoa, not so fast, big boy. We won't be needing *those* beauties again.' The manageress looked confused. 'Menopause, see?' I explained. 'So I thought, great. Refund or, at the very least, credit slip.'

'But this packet's partially open,' said the manageress, picking it up and peering at it.

'Ah yes,' I replied, 'but that, as I've just explained to this charming young sales assistant, 'is the *free* one.'

'I'm sorry,' she said, handing me the packet back, 'but it doesn't work like that.'

'In that case,' I snapped, stuffing it back into my coat, 'I'll just have to find a young woman of childbearing age and, not to put too fine a point on it, use 'em up.'

I was being heavily ironical, of course. I hate waste, but not to the extent of splitting up with the one true et cetera.

Naturally, I debriefed Blaise when I got home.

'And there you have it,' I concluded. 'Three packets of condoms. No use to us.'

'Never mind about that now,' said Blaise, punching the cushions and generally manhandling the furniture. 'Bonnie phoned earlier. She's on her way.'

Bonnie! My beloved daughter. Coming to see her beloved dad. This was wonderful news. I reflected that I hadn't seen my little girl for some time – her choice, not mine – but all that was about to change.

'Tell you what,' I enthused, 'this is a wonderful opportunity to finish her book. It's the last thing she'll be expecting.'

Now, as Blaise is a successful author I'm normally wary of mentioning my own writing efforts. But when Bonnie was a toddler I'd started work on an illustrated story about Bonnie and, such was my meticulous attention to detail, I'd never got round to finishing it.

'Are you sure that's a good idea?' said Blaise, violently plumping a bean bag.

I waved all doubts aside.

'She'll thank me for it. Trust me. You think I don't know my own daughter?'

'Hmn,' said Blaise.

And she said it again when I showed her my work in progress.

See Soggy Bottom Baby.

See her spanking brand new potty.

'It started as a toilet training manual,' I explained.

'Hmn,' said Blaise, flicking through the pages.

'Sorry, what are you implying?' I asked.

'She's nearly seventeen,' she said. 'Are you seriously thinking of giving this to your seventeen year old daughter?'

'Well I've got to finish it first. And I think I've worked out how to do it. I've got to get her sitting on that blessèd potty.'

Blaise put her arms around me and held me close.

'Don't do this,' she sighed.

Professional jealousy? Two Writers In Same House Syndrome? Difficult to tell. I kissed her menopausal forehead and disengaged. There was work to be done.

And what work! I'm always a little bit in awe of professional writers. All those words. And all of them so carefully – *arranged*. I, of course, had the added difficulty of the illustrations, although I freely admit I have absolutely no talent in that department. And it certainly showed. But the words. *There* was the challenge. It's all very well to say 'Get her on that blessèd potty', but you've got to make it aesthetically pleasing. Connect the botty to the potty in 8 pages of seamless prose, one sentence max per page.

Easier said than done.

I'd read all the books on the subject. Character arcs. Motivation. Structure. I even had a sub-plot of the disintegrating marriage working away in the background. But unless you know what's going on in that toddler's head – forget it.

I realised early on that the sub-plot, or, should I say *main* sub-plot, was Chekhovian in its themes of love, loss, the passing of the old order and, for some reason, the desire to move to Moscow. That was the easy bit. But I had to think myself into the mind of the child. Did the potty, for instance, have symbolic meaning beyond its essential self? Was there a possible Holy Grail motif at work here? Or were we talking rites of passage? To be honest, the story had begun to assume the timeless relevance of ancient myth and I was wondering – aloud, apparently – if the film version would respect the integrity of the text when the doorbell rang.

I downed tools – my biro in this case – and leaped into action.

I had assumed that my ex-wife would be dropping little Bonnie off. Last time I'd seen Dolores, two decades of wedded bliss and a nervous breakdown had taken their toll.

I opened the door.

'Dolores,' I gushed. 'You look positively youthful.'

'Hi Dad. Love the grey rinse.' And with that Bonnie brushed past me into the flat.

Blaise didn't seem as surprised as I was at the growth spurt. Apparently young people are like that these days, and my immediate thought was 'I hope they get on together, Bonnie and Blaise'. I know what women are like, and I didn't want them fighting like tomcats. But I needn't have worried.

'Wow,' said Bonnie as soon as she saw Blaise. 'It really IS you. The FAMOUS AUTHOR! My friends will be sooooooooo GUTTED!'

And before I had time to correct her on the grey rinse front, Bonnie had entered Blaise's study – out of bounds to *me*, I hasten to add – and was shrieking and giggling and referring to pretty well everything in there as AWESOME.

I heard all this from the safety of the bathroom. Bonnie had seen fit to close the study door on my face and I was getting used to the fact that her bonding with Blaise had gone better than I'd hoped. I was about to tear myself away from the bathroom mirror with the reflection that my hair was indeed verging on Hint of Gray, when Blaise's mobile rang. The shrieks and giggling stopped.

Silence for a moment.

Gray, I mused. Gravitas. Same Latin root? I never did find out.

Next thing I heard Blaise's door open.

'Just stay where you are,' she bellowed into her mobile. 'I'll be right over.'

I came out of the bathroom.

'Your mother,' I said. I wasn't asking. I knew it was her mother. 'Don't tell me. She's been watching daytime television. She's seen yet another gadget. She's bought it and, yet again, she's got herself stuck.'

'It's her new indoor ski lift,' sighed Blaise. 'It's stuck halfway up the stairs and she can't climb down.'

'I'll get my coat,' I said.

'I don't think it's time for you to meet Mother yet,' said Blaise and, turning to Bonnie, 'She has issues with your father.'

'Join the queue,' muttered Bonnie.

They both giggled. Queue? I thought. What queue? But I said nothing, and soon I was consoling myself with the fond thought that this would give me an excellent opportunity to finish Soggy Bottom Baby. Perhaps even colour in the pictures.

I waved them off, went back into the flat, and was just passing Blaise's study when I noticed that the internet had been left on. Another drowned polar bear, I chuckled, and ventured in to switch it off.

But just as I reached for the mouse my eye was caught by the screen.

myincrediblycomplicatedlifedotsomethingdotsomething

I knew the feeling.

I was soon drawn in, seduced by the artless prose and appalling punctuation. What is it with kidz these daze? Having said that, I must admit I found the energy refreshing and unintentionally comic.

I was just thinking that, in spite of the writer's best efforts, the character known as Dysfunctional Dad was coming across as the epitome of cool, when one of those chat line messages popped up.

'U still there?' it read.

Hmph. I wasn't too impressed with that.

'Me still here,' I typed wittily.

Or so I thought.

'Me still here 2. Like, wot's happnin?'

Right. That was it. The wit of my riposte had been lost on the recipient, and it awakened the traditionalist in me, that long dormant hungering for spit, polish and blue blazers that lurks beneath my louche exterior.

'Now look here,' I replied.

And I was off. I began my dissertation with a brief defence of one endangered species, the transitive verb, which segued neatly into a witty funeral oration for another, the subordinate clause. I then broadened my elegiac rant from the particular to the general – grammar; rules of – before getting to the nub of the problem, in which I bemoaned, with much flailing of arms and spittle in the grand rhetorical tradition of Cicero and his ilk, the absence of Latin on the school syllabus.

I double checked my message for typographical errors, pruned the central section of some of its more fanciful asides, and clicked *send*. I foolishly expected a considered response. 'U on somefink?' was not that response.

But enough of my Utopian visionary side. Tempus was fugiting fast. I still had to finish Bonnie's story and my idea for the final frame, some time later, was simplicity itself. Soggy Bottom Baby plonks her botty on the potty. Perfect. Well, almost. She's still wearing her nappy. This allowed for a follow-up and, depending on the success of the franchise, a possible series. I chuckled wildly to myself at the sheer giddy joy of being a tax exile, and had just settled down with a set of crayons for the all-important visuals when the ladies returned.

Bonnie headed straight for Blaise's study. Seconds later, she let rip with a wail of blood-chilling intensity, of almost heartbreaking anguish. Catastrophe! I thought. She's impaled herself on the swivel chair!

I raced to the rescue, but the cause of her outburst, it turned out, was slightly less fatal. Bonnie's online pals, it seems, had merely questioned her sanity.

Blaise, who had followed at a more leisurely pace, gave me one of those odd looks that she reserves for, well, *me*. She then clapped her hands with possibly forced jollity.

'Tell you what,' she said brightly, 'why don't you two spend some quality time together. Go for a coffee. And I'll sign some books for Bonnie's friends.'

Bonnie, however, seemed reluctant.

'Oh, come on, Bonnie,' said Blaise. 'What can possibly happen between here and the coffee shop?'

'You don't know Dad,' sulked Bonnie.

Blaise sighed.

'Oh, but I do.'

But Bonnie was off.

'We were at the beach, right? And he was just wearing these – '

Words failed her.

'Bathing trunks?' I suggested helpfully.

'I mean *everything* was showing,' wailed Bonnie.

'Surely not *everything*,' said Blaise.

'Okay. Right,' said Bonnie. 'Well maybe not *everything*. But *everything else*.'

Blaise, my love and my defender against all attempts at character assassination, sighed deeply.

'Well never mind about that now,' she said. 'But why not go anyway?'

And she thrust Bonnie's coat at her and bundled us out of the flat.

Bonding would come at the coffee shop, but first Bonnie wanted to pop into the chemist for, as she put it, 'women's things'. I waited at the counter and gazed upon her in wonder as she rifled the shelves. 'Women's things.' My little girl.

But not so little any more. She had metamorphosed, transmogrified, grown – that's the word! – into a beautiful young woman. And I? Well, time perhaps to think of a subtle tint.

I was toying with the idea of the self-applied blond streak when I spotted the manageress eyeing me from the safety of the cash register. Time to build bridges, I felt. I puffed up with pride as a heavily laden Bonnie bore down on the till.

'Aren't they just beautiful at that age,' I beamed, producing my credit card. 'So young. So lovely.'

Bonnie plopped her basket down on the counter.

The manageress, however, had eyes for me alone.

'You ought to be *ashamed* of yourself,' she hissed. 'People like you' – and she paused for maximum effect – 'disgust me.'

As I left the shop and went in search of Bonnie – so like her mother – I reflected that I probably wouldn't see her again for several years.

But as Blaise, my love and my soul mate, pointed out over steaming mugs of cocoa as we sat in bed that night, it would give me plenty of time to colour in her book.

Visit

Aimee Campbell

Ann stood at the cooker stirring the pasta so it wouldn't stick to the bottom of the pan. Steam rose from the bubbling water and she felt it attach to her cheeks.

'Look,' Jim said. He stood at the sink scrubbing a bowl.

'What?'

She picked a piece of pasta out and bit into it to see if it was ready. Water dribbled out of the middle and burned her tongue.

Jim nodded his head toward the window. Ann couldn't see anything apart from the guy who always stood and smoked across the way.

'The roof.'

'Oh.'

Her eyes scanned upwards and she saw a man walking on the roof. He moved clumsily, almost nervously. The tiles were wet in the early evening light.

Her stomach tightened.

'Did you put the garlic bread in?'

'Shit. No.'

She was just about to pull the bread from the freezer when there was a knock at the door.

'Did you hear that?' Jim turned to her.

Suds from his hands dribbled onto the lino.

'What if it's... ?'

'It won't be. Not at this time.'

She went to the front door. Maybe they would go away if they thought no-one was home. They knocked again, this time more gently. Pressing her ear to the door she heard two voices talking.

She opened the door. A teenage girl stood with a little boy.

'Is Des in?'

'No, there's no Des here sorry.'

The girl wore a black puffy jacket which almost covered her hands. The boys nose was red from the cold and he held a bottle of juice. There were tracks of glue where the paper had been pulled off around the middle.

'Oh right, wrong door. C'mon Kyle.'

She pulled away but the little boy wouldn't move and began to cry. She tried to take the bottle from him but he wouldn't loosen his grip.

'For God sake.'

He let go of the bottle. It bounced and the juice poured out, darkening the stone floor.
'Sorry.'

The girl bent to pick up the bottle which had almost rolled down the steps.

The boy held the lid tightly. His eyes shone in the dull electric light of the landing.

'It's okay' Ann said. 'Don't worry.'

'Do you know if there's a Des in this close?'

The girl lifted the boy up in her arms so he sat on her hip. He seemed a little heavy for her to hold.

'I don't know. There's a young guy upstairs, I don't know his name.'

The girl smiled and dotted the boy on the nose lightly with her finger. He screwed up his face.

'Naw, Des is my Da. He's old. Well, no ancient old. A bit older than you. About fiftyish?'

'Oh right.'

'Look... you wouldny have a spare couple of quid would you? I need to get this wee man something for his dinner tonight.'

'Hold on, I'll be back in a minute.'

Ann left the door open and ran back into the kitchen to get her bag.

'Who was that?' Jim asked, wiping his hands on a dishcloth.

'A girl and a wee boy. Where's my purse?'

She dug deep into her bag and felt around.

'Why do you need your purse?'

'Nothing, I'll tell you in a minute.'

'You're mad, it's probably a scam or something. You know what these folk are like.'

'Shoosh Jim. The door's open.' She held a finger to her lips. The purse was right at the bottom of her bag. There was only a pound coin and a couple of coppers inside.

'Have you got any money on you?'

'You're kidding.'

Jim slipped his hand into his back pocket.

'This was supposed to be for my train in the morning.'

He clicked a coin onto her palm.

'I'll give you it back.'

She rushed to the front door.

'Here you go...'

They had gone.

She stepped out into the close and listened. It was silent apart from the wind stuttering through the gaps in the window on the landing below. The dark juice stain had almost been absorbed by the stone floor. She felt the coins now warm in her hand, and rattled them a little between her palm and fingers. The sound seemed to carry up to the top of the building.

She went back inside, closing the door quietly behind her with a click.

'What's up?'

Jim had already dished out the pasta and was breaking the garlic bread into two halves, the crumbs scattering across the floor.

'Och, nothing.'

'Did you give them the money?'

'Aye.'

Still life

Joe McInnes

Me an ma Da wer sittin in the livin room. Him readin his Sunday Mail an me drawin a bowl ae fruit. When I got home he wis in the kitchen makin his Sunday breakfast, bacon, egg, sausage, black puddin, the works. I wisnae hungry but he kept shoutin in tae see if I wanted someten so I told him tae make me a roll on tottie scone an brown sauce. That wis wan ae the things that bugged me aboot ma Da, he never took no for an answer. I don't know, mibbe aw Da's are like that. But sometimes it can get on yer wick.

First, after ma Ma left, he went on a massive bender. Then aw ae a sudden he stopped drinkin aw together an went on a health kick. He started buyin lots ae fruit an veg an goin for walks, tritae get his act together. A couple ae times he even went swimmin. But wance he realised she wisnae comin back he more or less settled in tae his old self. Though he did manage tae stay aff the drink an that's a bit ae a miracle wance ye think ae it. An he kept on buyin fruit an veg even though he didnae eat it hisel any more.

It came tae me as I wis drawin the bowl ae apples an bananas, that if I raised ma picture plane I'd bable tae draw him in profile an he mibbe no notice. He'd still think I wis workin on the still life.

So I decided tae give it a go. I began by drawin a spherical shape for his heid, restatin the line till I wis satisfied. Then half way doon his heid I marked the eye level an ran a line doon tae the bottom ae his chin tae use as ma basic unit. That's just someten ye dae at the start ae a drawin tae get yer proportions right. When I wis first learnin tae draw portraits I used a graph divided intae aw different sections. It wis good for workin oot what goes wher on somedae's face. Like how the eyebrows sit at the bottom ae the skull an line up wi the top ae the ear kind ae thing. I'm tellin ye I must ae drew thousands ae they graphs. It comes in handy at first but after a while ye have tae discard it. Ye don't want yer drawin tae become too mechanical.

Ma Da wis wearin specs since he wis readin his Sunday paper but I drew the eye in as if he wisnae. I concentrated on the curve ae his eyelid before drawin the shape ae his iris. Wi ma rubber I erased a tiny highlight an used a B5 tae make his pupil darker. Even though ma Da wis readin his paper his eyes looked kind ae sad an at wan point I thought he wis gonnae burst oot greetin.

Ye ok Da? I asks.

Aye, he says. How what's a matter?

Nothin, I goes. I'm just wonderin if ye're ok.

I'm absolutely fine, he goes.

I moved on tae drawin his nose. Basically a nose is just a triangle shape, curved at the top in profile. I started tae fill in the outline ae his specs sittin on the bridge ae his nose. Ma Da's got a wee pudgy nose, even though he wis never intae boxin an is forever goin on aboot bein a pacifist. Next I drew a line between his lips an tucked it in at the corner ae his mouth. His bottom lip stuck oot like a big wean. I toned in beneath his lip tae catch the shadow an softened it up at the edges. Wance more I touched in the highlights wi ma rubber.

Even though it wis aboot one o'clock in the afternoon ma Da wis still wearin his housecoat. It wis an old brown thing an he had the collar pulled up roon his neck. Every time I magine ma Da he's wearin that housecoat. I drew in the jawline from his chin tae the bottom ae his skull. Tae get the position ae his neck I magined a line runnin diagonal from his eyebrow tae the front ae his neck an another wan comin from the top ae his heid for the back.

Most people magine the ear disnae count for much but see if ye don't get it accurate the whole drawin disnae look right. The bottom ae the ear lines up wi the bottom ae the nose, or the space between the nose an the top lip. Like I told ye the top ae the ear usually lines up wi the eyebrow. But member, it's no a science, everybody's different. Cause ma Da's heid wis tilted forward tae read his paper it made it that wee bit more tricky. But wance I got the alignment right it wis just a matter ae lookin an seein.

Hey you, ma Da shouts. Are you drawin me?

I didnae think ye'd notice, I pulled the sketchpad intae ma chest.

Aw Mhari, look at me, he goes. I'm a sight for sore eyes.

It's only a portrait Da, I goes.

Ye should ae told me an I'd ae put on a shirt.

It's no important what yer wearin, I says.

Show me, he says.

I'm no finished yet, I goes. I've still tae draw yer hair.

Sake Mhari, he goes. For aw I've got.

Just keep readin yer paper an pretend no tae notice, I says.

Ma Da tritae make oot he didnae mind bein baldy, but wance ye see photos ae him when he wis young he wis a good lookin guy. I began tae wonder if Danny would lose his hair wance he got older. I started tae think aboot last nite an it felt aw warm in ma belly.

I'd woke up first an gave Danny a shove an told him I had tae get back tae the party.

I need tae make sure no tae miss Janie, I says.

Long dae ye think we've been sleepin for? he wis rubbin his eyes.

I'm no sure, I says. But its light ootside.

He put his arm roon me an tritae kiss me but I wriggled free an told him I had tae get a move on. Don't get me wrong, I wanted tae kiss him but I wis feart ma breath might ae been stinkin.

Wance we arrived back at the party Janie wis sittin in the livin room wi a few other stragglers. She wis drinkin a Red Bull an they wer aw sittin talkin.

So the love birds decided tae return, she goes wance she seen me an Danny.

Wher's Billy? I asks.

He fucked off, she goes, pure pissed aff.

Danny didnae hang aboot for long either an wance me an Janie walked roon tae the bus stop she couldnae wait tae give me aw the gory details.

We did it, she says. We had sex.

I cannae really explain but I felt a wee bit jealous. But then she started greetin, tellin me how after it Billy had just ignored her.

It wis as if he couldnae wait tae get away from me Mhari, she says.

Don't let it upset ye Janie, I says. The guy's an idiot.

She wis dead quiet on the bus goin home. I thought it wis cause she wis comin doon aff her ecstasy. I must admit I wis feelin a bit hungover masel. We got aff at the shops an walked up tae her hoose so I could get changed.

Can I tell ye someten Mhari? she says wance we got tae the bottom ae her close.

Course ye can, I says.

That wis ma first time, she goes.

I didnae no what tae say. Janie wis always braggin aboot havin sex wi bhoys. I knew most ae it wis an exaggeration. I mean I am her best pal. But I would never ae thought she wis still a virgin. She looked at me as if she wanted me tae say someten. But I'm no exactly an expert masel.

Don't worry, I told her. It gets better wi time.

So what aboot you an that bhoy, she began tae cheer up a bit. Are ye gonnae see him again?

Danny hadnae asked for ma phone number. I wisnae too bothered cause his sister only stayed up the road from me an I felt sure I'd bump intae him again at some point. When I thought aboot him I began tae get butterflies.

Are ye no finished yet? ma Da interrupted me. I'm burstin for the toilet.

Nearly Da, I goes.

I'd made him look pure baldy cause I wisnae concentratin. I tritae fix it but ended up makin it worse.

Let me see, he got up an came roon behind ma chair.

Sake Mhari, I look like a sad old man.

I wis tryin tae show yer emotional side.

The Edison Portable Boiler

Juliet Lovering

It was years before he would completely abandon the belief that it was a living thing. It stood steadfast at a sturdy cubic meter and when it was full and operational it weighed well over a ton. Two cast iron handles gave the only suggestion of mobility but in twenty years it hadn't moved an inch. It was positioned at the apex of a triangle between the kitchen and the outhouses and was the simmering embodiment of Presbyterian excess.

He would stand on a stool and tip the potato peelings into the vast belching broth, offering scraps as appeasement. Everything went in. It was his part in a bargain he hadn't agreed to and didn't understand; the lack of clarity only made the contract tighter. When he passed empty-handed it was always at a self-imposed distance.

In the kitchen he set the scrap-pot down next to his mother who was flaking the meat from the hock for soup. Her fingers worked quickly, lubricated by the warm grease.

The shed door was ajar and the late morning light stopped just short of the immense spoked wheel. He halted in the doorway, conducting a clandestine survey from a respectful distance. When a quick glance over his shoulder confirmed he was alone, he decided on impulse to sit in the driver's seat. Squinting, his eye followed the axle along the full length of the machine to the high exhaust pipe that found its exit through the green bodywork. His arms embraced the broad steering wheel and moments later he was cranking up, purring and spluttering, using the weight of his body to lean in to imagined corners and straightening his legs to accommodate the earth's bumps. Recently, his father seemed straighter, taller even, and he understood.

The door opened and the light shone in. 'Out. Now.'

The whole family sat in silence with the pea and ham soup. There was no discussion between his father and older brothers about the work planned for the afternoon, no gentle mocking of each other's habits of speech, no feeding the dog under the table. As soon as they put down their spoons, and without being asked, he gathered in the dishes and cleared away the scraps. He disappeared outside, eager to dawdle, and consigned the leavings to the boiler. When the lid was lifted right back, and it had been a while since he had properly inspected it, it bubbled erratically, a barometer of his own inner turbulence. It would calm to a serene and level surface, and then one almighty dome of air would burst, spurting and whistling like a geyser. The ground reverberated and above this organic chorus, he heard his father starting up the tractor and driving off in the wrong direction: he would pass all the surrounding farms before he got where he needed to be.

He came chugging back at teatime in far better spirits, only one hand on the steering wheel and the other curled around a filthy towel. 'You should've seen their faces! Same colour as the bonnet, eh Big Green!' He dismounted with a wide grin, slapping the machine affectionately on the flank. 'Oi, Stirling Moss!' he called, beckoning him out from behind the boiler, 'I've a job for you.' He passed him the grubby bundle underarm, pausing briefly to catch the look on his face. 'You've to feed it up.'

He unwrapped the tiny pink body. It didn't wriggle or squeal like all the others in with their mothers; it was limp and tired. But he smiled, whispered to it and took it indoors. His mother sent him for milk from the goat and showed him how to feed it from the bottle without it going down the wrong way and into its lungs. They made a bed from a crate lined with newspaper, straw and a hot water bottle and he got down low on the floor to determine the most suitable draft-free spot. His enthusiasm waned at the mention of night feeds, but his brother chipped in that he was always getting up at night to pee anyway, so he didn't see what the problem was, and that was enough to silence any concerns.

Assisted by his reliable bladder, the piglet survived the week. Her meagre girth expanded and she found her voice. When there was a surplus, she had whey from the dairy and in time, she moved from goats' milk to pigswill. With a daily benefaction from the boiler she was thriving.

As the holidays extended in front of him, broad and long, he wanted to roam further than his charge would permit, and although he was enjoying ministering to the pig, he wanted to be with his friends, throwing stones and collecting things in jars. They could also add to their pocket money if they took the barrow round the village for swill. Despite confirming his mother as pig-sitter and leaving increasingly detailed and unlikely instructions, he struggled to get away. The piglet would follow. He would try to circumvent this, leaving while she was asleep, but she invariably woke with the crunch of his footsteps on the ground outside. In the end, he borrowed the dog's lead and took her with him. A proper pig in a poke, his brother joked.

Nobody much minded her tagging along. At a loose end one afternoon and astounded by the extent of one pig's appetite, they hit upon the idea of making her work for her food. They were all used to dogs and used the same methods, each of them keeping a handful of food in their pocket and rewarding good behaviour with a treat. Results came very quickly. Rather than having to seek out his friends, they called in on him, each with a new idea for a trick. By the end of the month, she could sit, lie down and offer a trotter.

After Sunday lunch they stayed around the kitchen table long enough for the feeling of over-fullness to dissipate.

'Do you want to help me oil the tractor?' his father asked.

'Uh huh. Come on Pinker' he called, and she trotted along behind.

'Pinker, is it?' he sighed. 'You don't name them son.'

He gave him the rusting oilcan to hold while he slid the door the full length of the tracks to let in the light. He pointed to the different parts of the engine and, unscrewing the cap, explained how the oil kept everything moving smoothly, prolonging the life of the vehicle. He held the bottom of the can with one hand and helped him direct the spout. 'That's it' he said, patting the seat, 'what about a wee ride, just to make sure the oil gets all round about?' It was impossible to suppress a smile as the machine bounced them around, and he giggled, giddy with the sensation of height, embarrassed at the childishness of the noise, but unable to stop.

Pinker was waiting by the boiler when they pulled back in, and as she saw him approach she adopted the sitting position as a gesture of obedience or goodwill. He rinsed out her bowl and filled it from the boiler's low-lying tap. The freshly poured slop was clearly irresistible and the sound of trotters clicking on the stone floor quickened to a skid. His father bent down and scratched between her ears.

'You're coming with me tomorrow.'

His mother was down on her hands and knees with the dustpan and brush, her back to the room, but he saw her lift the corner of her apron to her face. He experienced the injustice of it as a pain in his breastbone and an ache behind his eyeballs, and his anger was inflamed by the sense of his own powerlessness. After dinner, he spotted the key for Big Green and brushed it into the scrap pot with the leftovers. Elevated by the wooden stool, he lifted the lid and sent it down into the bubbling depths of the Edison Portable Boiler.

Critique of Violence

Zoe Coutts

As a school girl I spent one lunch break hunched under a toilet bowl, eyeing the toes of Choo and Louboutin. They were patent leather, embellished with grass and a thick mud crust. I worried their owners would hear me. My tin-wrapped sandwich lay untouched on the floor. I could barely breathe, let alone crackle a packet of crisps.

Cramped long past the bell, I ached for double Maths. Of course, they knew I was there. Who spent that long on the toilet? The girls at the mirror giggled and I strained to hear their tell-tale whispers. None came: only the stiff sound of mascara wands tugged through bristled lashes.

Later I performed a sweep of the bathroom, cheek to lino, before deciding it was safe to leave. Not daring to arrive halfway through Maths, I wandered the halls until the bell rang for Philosophy. Philosophy was easy and I liked the teacher. When I told her I was bored in class, she gave me essays by Walter Benjamin. My favourite is still the one about violence and law-making.

The others arrived and to my dismay I was seated next to Agnes. She smelled of cheddar. The girls on the back row tormented her, arm-in-arm. I offered her a tissue and suffered a kick to my chair leg. That is why Agnes and I could never have been friends: we saw ourselves in each other and were repelled.

These girls were the laws of the school. Violence is what makes a law and violence is what sustains it. I thought about Benjamin's essay and my way was clear. A new law was forming. I fought the tang of bile and turned to face the gang.

'Her name's *Agnes*. Her mum must hate her. That's why she's fat.'

My trembling arm was added to the chain. After class, we circled the common room. I was the centre; the others braided my hair.

Neither 45 Nor 1

Harry Giles

Two pernicious numbers are being trumpeted in the wake of Scotland's independence referendum.

The first number, 45, refers to the (rounded up) percentage of voters who stuck their X next to Yes. #the45 is the cry on social media, the six characters serving as a rallying point to rage, reminisce and consider what might happen next; its connection to another number, 1745, and its Jacobite rebellion is surely not a coincidence. These numbers are laden with grief, nostalgia, failure and longing. As a temporary rallying point, 45 has been effective; as a way to organise for the future, it's miserable and miserably lacking.

Technically, I am a 45er, but I have no desire to join the number. Nothing unites the 45 apart from their vote. I voted Yes as an opportunistic move to secure a few radical goals – the banishment of Trident and closure of Dungavel foremost – with some watercolour hopes for localised democracy and empowered movements in the background. In that, I have more in common with a Labour- and No-voting communist who seeks radical social justice (they exist!) than I do with an SNP- and Yes-voting nationalist who seeks only a strengthened Scottish nation (they exist too!) My goal is not a Scottish state: it is a radicalised people and a more just society.

The second number, 1, refers to One Scotland. While #the45 is the hashtag of the angry masses, #OneScotland is the banner of the political classes. It has been used by both Alex Salmond and prominent Labour campaigners to call for 'healing the wounds' between Yes and No in working for a better Scotland. In whose interests the wounds are healed and what actual politics are held in the promise of 'better' is quietly forgotten. While 45 asks us to rally together behind a lost cause, 1 asks us to forget our grievances and carry on with business as usual.

We are not one. The independence campaign succeeded in opening and exposing the many rifts and wounds in society: not just a vague resentment of Westminster and the political classes, but a focussed rage at income and health inequality, at ableism and exploitation in our work system, at outrageous patterns of land ownership, at institutionalised racism in media and immigration policy. The campaign did not open these wounds: it just gave voice to people, showing the world that the wounds were always there. These wounds cannot be healed by spin – One Scotland can only hide them from sight. These wounds can only be healed by a more just society.

Those of us campaigning for radical social justice have handed over our story to nationalism. We have allowed nationalists to argue that only a Scottish state can bring justice to Scottish people; we have allowed people to believe that the problem is solely Westminster, rather than a global neoliberalism of which Westminster is merely the most pustulent local extrusion. We should not now be campaigning for a Scottish state as the primary means to radical goals; rather, if a Scottish state is to come it must come through our struggle for social justice. Similarly, we cannot allow the ruling classes to paper over the cracks between us: there are women and men, there are workers and bosses, there are disabled and abled, there are divisions in society across which oppression works, and through which we can act in struggle and solidarity.

The Yes campaign was an uneasy alliance between a hundred different factions, temporarily and strategically united, each hoping for different goals from the same answer. That Yes must now fragment back into those factions – but this is a strength, not a weakness. We are more networked than ever before; we can be friends and comrades; we can go on each other's marches, support each other's occupations, sign each other's petitions. We do not need to unite behind the number of nostalgia or the number of amnesia. If we must be a number, 99 will do. But now we are many, together.

Jobs For The Dead

Tareq al-Karmy

I'm no warmonger or weapons trader.
But once this War is over I should become a junk dealer,
selling rifle barrels as artisanal flutes,
selling copper shell shrapnel to jazz music factories,
and the bones of tanks to Disney Land and kids amusement parks .
A war junk dealer, is what I should be;
selling the soldiers' skulls for church icons
and crumpled pictures that capture the last look of the dead,
arms amputated would be offered up to folk who'd lost theirs waving goodbye
at some harbour or an airport ,
or for those who had long dreamt of shaking hands with God someday.
I would sell the artillery tyres for wheelchairs,
the sniper rifle scopes for those who couldn't see far enough along the paths
that went astray.
And yes, I should become a rag and bone man in this last War.
But what about the armistice?
How will I buy it in the café of the generals?
I will sell whatever cannot be sold so that I can build an ants nest
for me and my three children to shelter in
for that final War which is making my eyes sneeze with its dust already.

Translated by Rym Nouria & Henry Bell

'I think there is always in me a sense of loss, an inability to believe in something I would very much like to believe in and which I once did. And that can be quite strange – unsettling – because it's almost an inability to believe in my own past'

The Gutter Interview
Kei Miller

The Gutter Interview: Kei Miller

Kei Miller is a poet, novelist and essayist. Born in Jamaica in 1978 he now lives in London. His poetry has been shortlisted for awards such the Dylan Thomas Prize and the Scottish Book of the Year. His fiction has been shortlisted for the Phyllis Wheatley Prize, the Commonwealth Writers Prize for Best First book and has won the Una Marson Prize. His recent book of essays won the 2014 Bocas Prize for Caribbean Literature (non-fiction). In 2010, the Institute of Jamaica awarded him the Silver Musgrave medal for his contributions to Literature. Kei has an MA in Creative Writing from Manchester Metropolitan University and a PhD in English Literature from the University of Glasgow. His 2014 collection, *The Cartographer Tries to Map a Way to Zion*, was shortlisted for the Costa Prize, and won the Forward Prize for Best Collection.

Gutter: First of all huge congratulations on winning the Forward Prize. It's well deserved. I think to some people it felt like a bit of a Glasgow win too. Even though you've left, do you still feel part of Scottish literature, or are there already enough claims on your identity?

KM: I'm glad it felt like a Glasgow win. So much of the book was written there, in my little flat (well...I guess it wasn't that little) which I miss terribly. This might feel strange to say, but I've never felt a part of Scottish Literature. I felt a part of Scotland, and of Glasgow in particular, but never of Scottish Literature which is such a bigger thing and quite frankly my work wasn't participating in those particular conversations or working through Scottish identities, etc. I never felt the compulsion to join that talk even while my students participated in it and I encouraged them and challenged them, but that has never been my own identity to work out or work through.

Gutter: On the subject of identities, some of the coverage of the Forward prize focussed on your background, rather than your poetry; and you've written before about the danger of 'minority' poets being 'nervously applauded but silently dismissed.' I recently saw Maya Abu al-Hayyat telling an audience 'I don't want to be a Palestinian, I want to be a poet!' Do you feel like there's a tension there in how the press have responded to you?

KM: Yes, those larger questions of identity and how it intersects with the art we create, hmm, it's a conflicting one. I have a lot of sympathy for Maya Abu al-Hayyat's position; many of my friends who write from the Caribbean have expressed similar sentiments. But I think in accepting that, we accept that to be a Palestinian or Caribbean writer is to belong to a small ghetto. There is something about accepting the label as a limiting one that worries me. And so, personally, I've never shied away from being a Jamaican or Caribbean or black poet. It says a lot about the material that I'm working with and I don't feel that makes the work any less worthy or any less rigorous.

Gutter: And how are you finding new found [literary] fame. Are you being stopped for selfies yet?

KM: A couple times – yes. But recently a few people at the Southbank waved me over and they had a camera in their hand, and I had this slightly diva thought – 'Oh God, this again!' And when I got there they were just tourists who wanted me to take their picture. So it seems the major thing that's changed is my false sense of ego rather than any real level of 'fame'.

Gutter: Do you feel that you're a different writer in Glasgow, or in London, or Kingston?

KM: Hmm... not in any way I'm yet to notice. Especially because the work I've been writing has often been written between all these spaces, and others.

Gutter: One of the key aspects where your work seemed to thrive in a Scottish setting, was you relation to language in the contexts of Jamaica and Scotland, talking about the continuum of language, the slide between dialects. Having moved down to London, do you find that is more or less of a presence in your life and work than it was?

KM: Part of the move to London was actually to reconnect to the Caribbean.

You're right that in Scotland a lot of the language politics resonate with the language politics of the Caribbean. But London is the Caribbean and so rather than less I've been much more immersed in dialects and an even more elaborate slide between Jamaican English, Jamaican Creole, and a South London Black British accent.

Gutter: Is this sliding between different languages part of the reason you are such a productive writer? Do different registers require different forms? Is there a key factor behind your productivity and range?

KM: No I don't think it's as neat as that at all. Almost any piece that I work on contains several registers and the right register won't always occur to me until I'm in the process of writing, or even rewriting it the 10th time. Perhaps the language variety of the Caribbean is partly responsible for why I became a writer in the first place, but who can really tell? For it isn't like everyone in the Caribbean is a writer. I guess writers are just inevitably interested in language and the dynamics of language and as I'm from the Caribbean I'm primarily interesting in those language dynamics.

Gutter: When you're working, how do you know what's a poem, or a short story, or a novel? How do you distinguish between your different writing?

KM: That's become easier over time. In poetry I'm simply not interested in narrative. *The Cartographer Tries to Map a Way to Zion* pretends that it's built around a kind of journey or narrative, but if you think about it, it's really not. What happens? What is the plot? There isn't any. And the poems themselves usually stay fixed on one moment that it is reflecting on or scalpeling through language. And when I do that, explore something with rhythm and with language, but without plot or story – I know it's a poem. And those things with plot then they are stories or novels, and when I feel my most polemic, well then that obviously becomes an essay. I happily allow the genres to infect each other, but I think I have a clearer sense these days of what my overall objective might be and therefore what genre each piece of writing ought to fit in.

Gutter: In 'XVII' you contrast the nyabinghi beat with the iambic pentameter, perhaps placing one as indigenous or natural, and another as colonial – though both are supposed to be heartbeats. How similar are these rhythms and how much of your literary education and upbringing would you say was colonial and how much was not?

KM: I actually hope it didn't suggest that... well not exactly. While Rastafari is actually one of the few indigenously Caribbean religions, the larger question of indigeneity and the Caribbean is a vexing one and I'm careful never to suggest that the Afro-culture of the Caribbean is any more indigenous than its European culture. In fact, the opposite would be true. In the Caribbean the opposite of 'colonial' is not 'indigenous'. We were all transplanted there – white, black and Asian cultures. But sorry, that's a long disclaimer. I would say the vast majority of my education was what you might call colonial. But I

didn't think of it in those terms. It was just education and culture and in fact a lot of it came from several different places at once and to parse some as colonial and some as 'whatever the opposite of colonial is' wasn't something that occurred to me until much later.

Gutter: *The Cartographer* seems often to be about dismantling oppositions, or shifting the perspective on binaries. How central is that theme to your politics and poetry?

KM: That might be more central to my personality than to my politics. I do distrust binaries but I think the reasons for that are quite obvious. It's not for the sake of distrusting them, it's because they're actually simplistic and oftentimes wrong. I think the job of the writer is to make the world more complicated, not more simple. To make the world more simple is bad faith and lazy. The world is a wonderfully extraordinary and beautiful place if we stop to consider and work through the messiness of it all.

Gutter: In terms of 'mapping to zion' and the cadences of your poetry suffused in the King James Bible do you feel a longing for religion? And is it for a Calvinist faith? A Church of God one? A Rastafarian one? Something else?

KM: I think there is always in me a sense of loss, an inability to believe in something I would very much like to believe in and which I once did. And that can be quite strange – unsettling – because it's almost an inability to believe in my own past, or an inability to believe in something that's still in the centre of myself and that forms who I am. So this longing for religion comes out, but what kind of religion? I couldn't tell you that. I don't know.

Gutter: In the poem 'Shotover' – which is one of my favourites – you write 'when victims live long enough they get their say in history.' This reminded me of the South African theologian Farid Esack who wrote that liberation theology was about 'reclaiming authenticity from the victors.' In Esack's context this meant a radical rereading of the Qur'an against colonialism and patriarchy and in some of your poems you have in different ways been re-writing the bible, or re-telling your life using a framework from the bible. Why do you think it's so much a part of your writing?

KM: The bible shapes much of the Caribbean. Even Rastafari which sets itself up as the antithesis of the 'whiteman's religion' is very much rooted in the King James Bible. So that kind of framing I almost take for granted. I know it must seem quite strange here, or even exotic, but I don't think reaching for that language – a biblical language – in both secular and religious settings means terribly much in the Caribbean, these ways in which in our everyday speech we reinscribe or rescribe or unscribe whole sections of the bible, it's all very natural, very commonplace. It is simply the language that is out there.

Gutter: You said of winning the 2004 Manchester Poetry slam: 'I am ashamed to

have won that prize, and truth be told, I am also ashamed that I am ashamed.' What did you mean? And do you see a firm separation/ hierarchy between 'page' and 'performance' poetry?

KM: I don't see a firm separation. There is obviously a separation but it isn't firm. My own poetry stands resolutely at that porous boundary where things bleed into each other and the oral and the scribal infect and affect each other. But if I'm honest to myself, the place where I've always wanted to prove myself and declare myself is on the page. Perhaps that means, for better or worse, and for all kinds of reasons that seem to compromise the politics that I stand for, I end up holding on to a hierarchy that I find objectionable.

Gutter: As you blog widely about homophobia and misogyny in Jamaica, but are also read in the UK, do you worry that people might use some of what you write as a justification for a bigoted view of Jamaica?

KM: No – funnily enough I don't worry so much about that. It's hard to explain why. You see, I do think a lot of what goes on in Britain and America as concern for Jamaica's homophobia really is a kind or racism, this strange first world contempt for those poor natives and their backward savage ways. I would never want to give ammunition to that, nor do I think I do. I don't critique Jamaica from a place of contempt and my blogs are usually around a specific issue and addressed to specific people who often times take the time to respond, and in that I don't mind people in the UK eavesdropping on a conversation in the Caribbean and observing that these things are being challenged and talked about on the ground. In fact, maybe at best it gives a model for a more appropriate shape that their concerns might take.

Gutter: Do you think that being an immigrant is harder now than it was when you first came to the UK?

KM: Well I object to the word 'immigrant'. I am certainly someone who has migrated, but 'immigrant' seems to me an increasingly racialised word. Meaning, someone else from the UK say, in a reverse position, having moved to the Caribbean for an academic position, then they would be an 'expat', not an immigrant. The term 'immigrant' seems to require some kind of attitude of perpetual gratitude and subservience from me and who can stomach that? But as something of a foreigner living in the UK, is it harder? I'm not sure. I'm much more aware of the politics of my place here and that place being increasingly fragile, but also with time you naturally are much comfortable about your place. It's only in the last year that I've been comfortable to think of myself as British. Never Scottish or English mind you – I can't hold on to a UK national identity. But the larger umbrella of British – that actually fits in a strange way. But are things harder? No. On a day to day basis I think it's pretty much just as sometimes-welcoming and sometimes-benignly racist and sometimes-warm and sometimes-cold as it's ever been.

From A *Paraphrase of Dante's Sublime Comedy*, Canto 9

Alasdair Gray

Dante, led upward by his angelic sweetheart Beatris, has just been told by Justinian, the Christian Emperor, how God created the Roman Empire to pacify the world by force of arms, then crucify Christ to make Roman Christianity universal, before destroying Jerusalem. The first verse of this canto is still in the voice of Justinian, followed by four in which Dante tells how the Emperor's explanation of the Crucifixion puzzled him, followed by Beatris's explanation. Her name should be pronounced with three syllables: Be-a-tris.

'To Heaven's greatest height now praise our God
who gloriously brightens with his rays
good hearth-fires everywhere on holy days!'

So sang that bright soul, dancing as he sang,
    that ruler who had striven to connect
    justice on earth and Heaven's government.

In happy play the other shining souls
danced with him too, until like shooting stars
they disappeared by being far away

and left me brooding in perplexity.
    I well knew Beatris could quell my doubts
    so *Tell her! Tell her!* sounded in my head,

but reverence had overcome my tongue.
    Parts of her name (be, is) still strike me dumb.
    She did not leave me thus, for with a smile

that would have cheered a burning man she said,
    'You do not see why justice should demand
    vengeance upon revenge for ancient sin?

Listen and hear true doctrine straight from me.
   Adam, the only man not born but made,
   was given all good things men can enjoy

but could not bear one curb upon his will
   so damned himself and we who spring from him.
   Long ages passed before the Word of God

descending, worked to free us from this ill.
   By one act of amazing love God took
   body with we who have rejected Him,

became a sinner too, deserving death
   like me and you, and in Gethsemane
   sadly embraced that foul necessity,

accepting Roman law so none can say
   our Maker never felt our suffering.
   If human need for death is understood

indeed Christ's death was good. If we respect
   His righteousness, nothing was more unjust.
   From that great act came opposite effects –

Christ's death desired by God *and* Jewish priests,
   for which earth quaked and Heaven opened wide,
   and Solomon's great temple was destroyed.

I fear your thoughts are fankled in a knot
   you can't untie. Although my words are clear
   why God redeemed us thus is dark to you.

Brother, it is dark to everyone
   with minds unripened by the sun of love.
   I'll say it all again in other words.

God's excellence is never envious,
so all the souls he makes possess like Him
   eternal life, like Him, freedom of choice.

These gifts are lost by people choosing sin.
Adam and Eve disobeyed God; believed
rejecting God would make them equal him,

thus they exchanged eternity for time.
   Justice cannot ignore so mad a crime
   which all folk born of women re-enact,

so gaps between ourselves and Paradise
   are far too big for penitence to fill
   by any single act of human will

though penitence is certainly required.
   Only a miracle could reconcile
   justice with mercy, and at last it came.

God's overflowing goodness made His Word
   human, like us; offered new birth, new life,
   eternally to all who follow Christ

and grasp their cross – forgive who do them wrong –
   love enemies and promise not to sin.
   What better thing to save us could God do

than show all people how we ought to live?
   I see you want more news of sacred things,
   a thirst I'll satisfy before you ask.

What troubles you is instability.
   God made the earth and water, fire and air
   so must have made them pure as Paradise –

pure as these starry spheres, this shining space
   through which we soar. Why on earth do all things
   Change, age, sicken, die and rot? Here is why.

Our God himself did not directly make
   all of the world below. Live plants and beasts
   are generated in His elements

by things he made before. Sunlight is one.
   Yet on the sixth day of the Genesis
   He breathed His own soul into human clay.

All other earthly life will suffer death.
   Men, women are the great exception,
   created by His love to love Him back

eternally, after resurrection.'

Aleph-Beth

Samuel Tongue

Eve   Adam
          the first shamans
glistening in snakeskin   singing
to snakes   twisting
like snakes
          electric animals   speaking animals
ribbed bodies already hieroglyphs
          writhing writing
          in the dust under the tree
     aleph א an ox-head or stag-head
                              antlers swaying heavy in the dance
an animal letter
               hoof-prints in their soft brains
     already tracks of thought
and in the beginning   *beth* ב a blueprint for a dwelling
          to be bricked once the mud has baked
     and the dust has settled
                              in the cool of the evening
God walks through the garden
               and reads the shaman Eve
                         reads the shaman Adam
     as animals that say animal (*animot*)
               who know they are animal
          and know too much

Six Aphorisms on the Nature of Language

Stewart Sanderson

(Adapted from Flaubert)

Language is like a cracked pot on which we beat out tunes for bears to dance to, but with which we seek to move the stars to pity.

*

A cracked pot is like a tune for bears to dance to, with which we seek to move the

stars to pity.

*

A tune is for bears to dance to, with which we seek to move the stars to pity.

*

A bear is to dance, and so we seek to move the stars to pity.

*

A dance is to seek to move the stars to pity.

*

A star is to pity.

Eight poems from *Silly Billies*

Cheryl Follon

Snow

It starts as plinky flecks then turns to big wet
slaps on the window. Snow says, you ever
spread a snow blanket down and done algebra
under the big snow tree? You got no style, no
nothing. A mouth like a giraffe. How come
you're scared of turnstiles? Come on, it says,
let's play snow ball.

Paper Flowers

Just when the hash smokers are going out to
shoplift Scotch eggs, and the neighbour is
drinking milkshake, paper flowers is making
paper flowers – endless strings of the things for
an endless cycle of births, deaths and marriages.

Magnesium

So I kept 20,000 servants with the sole purpose of doing nothing more than tickling my feet – but when the magnesium was brought out in its white box no-one was allowed to touch it – not even me.

Manners

The master of the desert and grasslands – kingdom of date and fig and camel, as far as the eye can see – 2,000,000 camels and just as many foot soldiers, camps collapsed and set up 40 miles on. And her – legendary baths, rose oil, flannels of milk, black and white eunuchs, a trail of pink petals falling out behind her while she walks. He was brought up to lead all men, and she was brought up to do the same. On the burning gold of the Eternal Gold Palace the sound of two voices... No, please, let's take my horse; no, I insist – let's take *my* horse...

Crème Caramel

The annual crème caramel eating competition is in full swing: where one man eats his weight in crème caramel and takes the yellow gold medal.

Rain

There was no official name for rain for a long time – it just started falling and folk let it get on with the job. It possibly was named when kids said for the first time ever, 'tell us the story about Chicken Licken and his bad leg'. This happened and the rain kept falling. Someone tried to describe it, saying, part melon, part cockroach, part soup tureen. But it was no use and the rain just kept on coming and still does till this day.

Contrariness

My girlfriend treats me like dirt, and really enjoys it. She says it's down to her two-way split. She's the kind of girl who says 'as there's no-one here to give me oral I gotta read this boring magazine'. Or, 'I'm just so deeply aware of the grave, or maybe just a slave to my big clit'. That's the kind of girl she is – the words grave and clit in the same sentence. Her two-way split, she says.

Santiago

Mama said, let's move to Santiago, and we did. The buildings were close together making that city very dark, but the electric whiteness of tornado lollies and ice-cream eyeballs made up for it, and amongst that darkness it was the first place they found night owls.

Tightrope Walker

Kay Ritchie

(i.m. Alice Ernestine Prin – Kiki de Montparnasse
– 1901-1953)

no net below
just faces gaping
till she topples
through kaleidoscope reflections of herself
naked climbing stairs
dancing with a bear
hair bobbed comme un garçon
cheeks stained red geranium
pubes and eyebrows shaved
redrawn with burnt out matchstick
or whatever shade has caught her mood

they call her *La Reine*
the dadaists
      surrealists
           futurists
come to be amused
by her risque performance
describe her face as cat-like
her profile as stuffed salmon
her scent as chicory   Pernod
but she's Guerlain's 'L'HEURE BLEUE'

when she climbs on tables
lifts her skirts
shimmies shameless Chez Kiki
garter hose and more
they buy her hashish   red wine
paint her
      sculpt her
           film her

water-mirrored
smashed in glass
through flames
in sculpted wire

she is a Jean Cocteau
                Max Ernst
      Man Ray
a tightrope walker

dancing in the sky

On a Painting by Sang Jianguo

Shane Strachan

They take pictures of each other,
the dandelion clocks
around their feet.

Hair blows in the breeze
and seeds rise up
through tripods, legs
and tree trunks

parachutes caught
in the light
between them and her:

hand on hip, jacket sliding
down her shoulders,
staring at me
like a lens uncovered,
ready to shoot.

Ma Mither's Luver

George T Watt

A dauncit tae seduce him,
ma mither's luver faw luikit
at ma airms floatin mystikal
ma een baith innocent an pleadin
ma breists aneath the silken claith
caain oot tae be held,
tae feel his hauns sclim ower thaim
ma bellie supple an sensual
ma hurdies swayin like fertile corn
woven by ae hidden breeze
an hoo he langed tae possess me,
ma mither's luver.

An she watched an smiled like an edder,
her tung slitherin ower her lips
while ma virgin body gaed itsel
tae an orgy o sleekit aged een,
but the een that wanted me maist,
belanged tae ma mither's luver.

Entransit, owercam wi desire,
he'd hae gaed me ocht A wanted,
rubies, pearls, gowden whigmaleeries,
onything his desert kingsteid possessed,
but A dauncit tae ma mither's wish,
an hoo yon luik still haunts me.

Was A tae ken coveteous een cuid betray
a cheil faw held honour like a cruik
that aids ane ower roch grun?
Ma mither's lauch scraiches waein ma lugs,
but thay starin, crazed, akusin een,
still haud thair pooer atween me
an ma mither's luver.

The Miser's Sporran

George T Watt

A hae seen thay northern bens glintin
like ae thoosan whigmaleeries in the autumn sun,
siller coins hauden in ae miser's grip
faw's sleekit een lauchit at the puir,
cared nocht for the feeble o speirit
o the aged ailin and painfu, beleivin
nocht o thay frailties wuid er owercam him.

A hae seen ae million acres o blasted hather,
straunglin aa the breith oot o the laun,
whaur broch an auncient crannogs,
cairns an simmer sheilins, tell like the yairns
o the aul men faw sit in the ingle neuk,
mystic een retellin wi hertfelt pride
the annuls hidden deep waein thair conscience.

For ae million years thay straths
sang tae the vyces o weemen milkin the kye,
the birdies lauchit wi the bairns at pley,
file menfowk chyaved an luved an begat
some wi care an passion ithers wi callous weicht,
an weemenfowk wi thair smeddum, keppit
geinerations aunchored tae the laun.

But distant pooers decreed ainly the selfish fui,
weel heeled an enslaved bi greed,
shuid hae aa this laun an the hale weicht o government
wuid help thaim tae rid the laun o fowk,
for it maun be thairs tae despyle an neglekt,
an nae bairns lauchter, nae sang o simmer shuid brak
the silence, o the miser's sporran.

The voice, the tone,
the taste of the words
lingered in the mouth so
profusely, I dare not copy
them here. But I will re-
tell the story for you. Do
not get impatient with
me, and do not deem
the tale irrelevant.

Confessions of Kibar
Defne Çizakça

Confessions of Kibar
Extract from a Novel in Progress

Defne Çizakça

Everyone in Kuzguncuk knew The Biggest Library of Istanbul; on its entrance there was an arabesque that said, 'Step inside for books.' And in the hallway there was another: 'This is the house blessed by your rosy heels.' Kalliopi is the one who invited me into that library, Your Honour, and the second sign made me doubt I was clean enough to enter it.

At that point in my life, I was making the switch to a professional singer. It was not easy to transition from a beggar, to an *aşık*, and then on to a performer. Each step brought with it difficulties and boredoms peculiar unto themselves. I did not yet have the authority you currently see crowning my shoulders; I was only a young man then, clumsy and scared of life. Being an *aşık*, I had a kind of allowance to be a little out of the ordinary however, a little odd if you want to put it that way. And because I was also a good entertainer with Eastern stories, I was welcome to the salons of Istanbul even though I was poor. But the reason Kalliopi called me over that November day was not a musical matter.

She did not give explanations as we toured the house. Her skirts swooshed, and the light from the windows in those endless corridors was hushed yet warm. Kalliopi took out an old rusty key from her pocket and opened a door for me. There was a pinned map on the centre of a mahogany desk, and a fireplace, and row after row of tender looking books. Upon seeing the room a strange quiet fell upon me, Your Honour, like the prayer veil. Kalliopi had to wait for me to return to my senses. This was the room of the famed coffeehouse books.

She had called me over, Kalliopi said, not just to share this treasure of a room with me, which was marvellous as it was, but also because she had discovered a mystery in one of its collections. She wanted me to solve it. Nothing less than a murder, she whispered with squinted eyes, and quickly added, 'do not worry, it was centuries ago and the murdered was only a dwarf.'

Kalliopi handed the coffeehouse book to me. As I read, I fell in love with the elegance of the tale written in it, Your Honour, for a moment forgetting the event it was recounting. The voice, the tone, the taste of the words lingered in the mouth so profusely, I dare not copy them here. But I will re-tell the story for you. Do not get impatient with me, and do not deem the tale irrelevant. You ordered me to prove my innocence and the only way I can do it is by telling you of all that occupied my time in 1876. In this spirit I present the entry on the dwarf, in coffeehouse book number twelve, which sits right before you in its glass container, both witness and proof.

*

The story Kalliopi handed over to me was about a man the scribe referred to as 'Little Father,' whom, I reckon, must have been very short. The penman, who called himself 'The Orphan,' had met Little Father on a stormy night in the neighbourhood of Galata. He says a thunderstorm was setting the other side alight; raindrops were big and hot and scalded his skin. The Orphan saw Little Father staring into a blind alley named Hagalapoulos. The man's expression was pained; perhaps the Orphan even spotted tears in his unblinking eyes and so he moved towards him and saw that a man, another dwarf, had been hung from a lantern at the end of the alley. His neck was broken but not only that; the killers had carved out his shoulders and stuck candles in them that continued to burn despite the storm.

They freed the dwarf off the rope, they carried him to Little Father's home which was filled with precious stones and amber tables, divans of the softest velvet and bright coloured liquids bubbling in twisted vessels. They washed the dead. The Orphan felt his hands were useful, strong and worthy. He felt privileged to be in such a rich house even if it was because of a murder. Little Father found a pouch in the dwarf's convulsed mouth. When he untied it, red coloured dust sprinkled on to his pinkie. It burned and quivered with pain but Little Father smiled with tears running down his face. By morning the tip of his finger gave a metallic little tap when he rapped it on the table. It shone too, like something precious. Little Father asked the Orphan, then, whether he would want to journey across the hilly, golden steppes of Anatolia with him to see someone he had heard stories about, who would know what to do with this powder. If so, they would have to leave immediately.

Now, Your Honour, what Kalliopi wanted me to do with this story was not simple. She wanted me to find out who wrote it, which is something I could do since I was an *aşık*, she assumed. I also knew some of the booksellers that wind down the grand bazaar because I had begged there, although Kalliopi did not know that. I had places from where to begin, which on accounts of being a woman, Kalliopi did not. As a way to reward my further research, Kalliopi invited me to sing at the library. 'A small token of my gratitude,' she said. 'Singing here will elevate you to a whole other level Kibar. Plus, I am writing a book on *makams*, and not everyone can traverse them as easily as you do.'

I accepted the offer to sing immediately, but going on a quest for a murderer who must have died a century ago? Despite the good beginning to a strange story, I halted, Your Honour. My curiosity did not get the better of me, no. I had had my share of adventures in the streets of Istanbul, and was not interested in more trouble. It wasn't curiosity but the money Kalliopi handed over that made me say yes.

As I left the room with the coffeehouse books alongside Kalliopi, the bills snug in my undershirt, the offer to sing making my mouth water, I saw Perihan for the first time. She was reading in a room down the corridor, with a magnificent yellow bird sitting on her shoulders. She was so focused she didn't notice us as we walked past her. And then I was going down the stairs led by Kalliopi's swooshing skirts, with my scared little heart on which the image of a murdered dwarf had been planted.

*

With all good intentions, Your Honour, I tried to find out the truth about that poor little dwarf. But I couldn't even be sure of the year in which the story was written; the entry in question was not dated. The other writings in the coffeehouse book did not provide a clue either as there were centuries between them. Naturally, the tale was not signed; humble scribes do not use names as they write. So I returned some of the money Kalliopi had given me and told her that the trail had gone cold. I had not been able to satisfy her murder quest, but I certainly satisfied her other wish.

Kalliopi put me on a stool placed in a long corridor. She ordered me to sing. As I sang, serious looking, dark, handsome men passed us by. At times they applauded, at times they took a break from whatever it was they were doing and smoked a cigarette while sighing to my voice. Kalliopi wrote down feverishly. She interviewed me, asking me about my health, wondering whether I felt certain sentiments during certain *makams*, scrutinizing how I prepared myself for the high and low notes. I felt trampled on. After two months of this, she said I had now earned the right to sing for a select audience in the library and that is when I finally met Perihan.

Perihan Hatun had a big nose and sad eyes. I understand she had no idea Kalliopi had called me to the house to solve a murder. She told me she was glad I had been able to help Kalliopi with her *makam* book. 'I have another issue I need help with,' she said, and then took me with great ceremony to the very same room Kalliopi had taken me: the one that stored the coffeehouse books. She explained how this collection was unique as it covered a wide range of coffeehouses from Aleppo to Sarajevo, and from all the *vilayet* the Ottomans had ruled. I did not have the heart to tell her Kalliopi had already informed me of all this.

'I am going to share a secret with you that only three people in the world know,' she said and I grew scared. These three people were Perihan's deceased father, Kalliopi, and Perihan herself. She was sharing it with me because I was a vessel for Eastern Stories. 'I heard you know the fairy tales of the Yezidis, the Kurds, the Arabs, and the Druze,' she said. To please me she served a cup of coffee so filled with cardamom I screwed up my face.

A book lay open on the mahogany table between us, inside it an article of only a few sentences. She ordered me to read it:

The Granddaughter of Ma'an:

Born in the imperial palace of Istanbul sometime in the 1700s. Granddaughter of a prince executed by Sultan Murat IV for his revolts against the Empire. Daughter of Ma'anoğlu who was his only unkilled son. The granddaughter of Ma'an travelled far and wide, became a man, and turned copper into gold.

Perihan asked me if I knew any tales about the granddaughter of Ma'an. If I knew perhaps traces of the real person that had trickled down from mouth to mouth. Kalliopi had asked me to search for a murder, Your Honour, Perihan asked me to search for a woman.

She copied the article on a clean sheet for me: 'I have become lonely,' she said, 'I had hoped she would keep me company.'

I didn't know whether Perihan Hatun was referring to the woman mentioned in that old book, or to Kalliopi who did not raise her head to greet us when we walked by.

*

I collected whatever crumb I could find on this granddaughter of Ma'an. For the sake of Perihan I went and found Hayalci. You may already know him, Your Honour, he is now sitting at the second row, the one with the crimson kaftan. Even in cities far from here, in the land of Greeks and in the land of Arabs, his stories prevail. He is, despite this fact, the most humble man I know, and like me, Hayalci comes from the East.

I knocked on the door of the coffeehouse next to Aya Pantelemion. A Greek called Ioannis opened its chestnut door. The moment I saw Hayalci napping at the back of the room, I knew, Your Honour, that not only would Hayalci know of the girl Ma'an, he would tell her story better than any piece of writing ever could. When I asked him about her, he began to perform on a whim as the best of tellers do, very much aware of his own talents and of the fact that I hung on the charm of his lengthy eyelashes, and the tip of his tongue.

It seems that once upon a time, a long long time ago, when the Crusaders had begun storming our lands for gold, there appeared a people around Mount Lebanon whose destiny it was to repel these infidels. The girl Ma'an came from such a fine family. They were peasants on ordinary days, but once the wars began, they turned into fighters, better than the Turks, better than the Persians, incomparably better than the Arabs. They were a secretive people whose women wore long hats and who took the surahs of the Qur'an and twisted them into riddles like fairy tales. They were a people rumoured to have alchemy on their side. Their leader was a man called Ma'anoğlu; an olive skinned prince who built his castle on a hill overlooking the harbour of Jubayl. After fighting the Crusaders so bravely, there was no reason to excuse the Ottomans who had occupied these lands for years and the prince began his revolts against the ruling Turks in Istanbul.

For a while Ma'anoğlu seemed to ride the waves. Ottoman soldiers lost their path under an unknown sky, they got stranded in steep narrow valleys then died of heat and thirst, many were seduced by women so doe-eyed they could not be abandoned in the midst of deserts. But eventually Ma'anoğlu's luck ran out, and he was captured together with his three sons and brought to Istanbul. He thought of answers on the long journey to the imperial city. Had the Sultan asked him a question or two, he would have known how to elongate his time on this earth, the way Scheherazade had, but the Sultan did not ask him anything. Instead, with one nod Ma'anoğlu, and with another his first-born son were beheaded. A third nod, and Ma'anoğlu's second born died. One, two, three and the clan of Ma'an were all slaughtered in the garden of Topkapı, by an executioner whose axe struck with a base baritone *bismillah*. All of them, but one. This is where, Your Honour, fate interferes. For unknown reasons, Ma'an's last-born son was spared his life. Did the headsman have pity on the boy? Or did the Sultan change his mind in the last minute? All we know is that Ma'anoğlu's youngest heir survived. He grew up in the palace, and in time, became the right hand of the Sultan who had killed his father and two brothers.

The son of Ma'an had a daughter who was red of cheek, plump of lip, and cheerful of spirit. She grew up in the imperial harems, and was taught everything she knew by her father. Every day father and daughter sat together to read that family Qur'an from which they took out surahs only to change their meaning and in this way a father passed on everything he knew to his daughter. They studied philosophers and scientists, the effects of the planets on metals, transmutation into *al-Insān al-Kāmil*, the perfect person. And the scholars of the palace enjoyed stopping by and having their last coffee together, before retiring to their poor households for the night.

Storyteller Hayalci told me that this innocent girl escaped from the palaces the night she turned sixteen. The time had come to accomplish what her father had been teaching her, and what his poor decapitated father had taught him before that: the time had come for the daughter of Ma'anoğlu to turn copper to gold. And to do that, the girl Ma'an shaved her hair, put on a turban, and left the harems dressed as a man. She walked straight and proud out of those jagged city walls.

*

Each week I would update Perihan, Your Honour. On Wednesdays I gave concerts at the library. On Thursdays, after the evening prayer of *isha*, more often than not, we had milk with honey – the way children like it, with *lokum* to the side. Perihan would eagerly await me, she told me so herself. Neither Kalliopi, nor Perihan's husband Ruhi, would join our conversations. I doubt they ever knew about them.

Perihan always wore beautiful dresses that I had such an urge to touch: Bursa silk, Persian satin; she must have known all the Jewish sales women, I was certain of it. It did not take much to rouse her imagination. I would tell her long, slow and melodious tales that I embellished so as to spend more time with her. Perihan, in her turn, urged me to go ahead and discover more of the girl Ma'an.

The problem was that Hayalci could tell me nothing further, ask him yourself, Your Honour. When he could not complete the story Hayalci sent me off to another teller who told me a bit more, then he too stopped in the middle and directed me to another. In this way, hopeful and uncertain as a dog, I went from coffeehouse to coffeehouse. Always and only searching for the tellers who had a smell of the East at the back of their ears, and around their neck. Something earthy and spicy; a smell I too carried like a protective talisman.

It seems, Your Honour, the granddaughter of Ma'an travelled as an alchemist and experienced self-doubt on several occasions. There had been no good reason to escape the imperial harems where she would have grown old in rose smelling shadows. No man would have been allowed to touch her as she was an *emanet* rather than property, and upon old age she would have been married off to a man in a position to take care of her, one of the many palace teachers perhaps, the ones who were already, secretly, besotted with her. But the girl Ma'an did not like predictability. She would not have it, the way some people will not touch okra. This quality made her beloved by storytellers, which may be why they refused to write her story down for centuries. But the unpredictability also made her susceptible to the onslaught of djinns.

A woman must not travel such long distances alone, Your Honour. The Bible says as much and so does the Qur'an. The djinn's eventual intervention was inevitable and occurred on a rainy night prone to such slips, a night on which the granddaughter of Ma'an forewent the male bathroom of the caravanserai for the female. She lifted up her skirts to scoot, and before her, by the bucket she would soon fill with water to clean up after herself, she saw the child. The man-child.

Zümrüt was smaller than a midget. His hands, arms, and legs belonged to a four year old yet his face was covered with the thickest, blackest beard you could imagine. Half his face was taken up by piercing, blue-green eyes – which is why, Your Honour, he was named after an emerald.

First, the man-child was as surprised, and as scared, as the girl Ma'an. But soon he knew his luck. For you see, he could see a bit of the future but not all of it. He could steal gossip like breadcrumbs from the heavens, but not the whole story. He was a conduit between this world and the next, Your Honour, though not a stable one. So Zümrüt saw that Sultan Murat IV and the girl Ma'an would meet, and he saw that she would be gifted many treasures by that Sultan. But Zümrüt did not see the rest of their tale. Zümrüt chose the granddaughter of Ma'an based on the partial information he had. He promised to be her companion through it all, obedient and sweet. When the doubt on her face did not subside, he added, 'I will be yours whether you like it or not.'

Recognizing this iron will, the girl Ma'an looked at the man-child's feet and saw that they were pointed backwards and knew then: she had indeed met a djinn. Creatures of fire so powerful they had managed to spill from the Qur'an on to her Druze books.

*

For a while, the girl Ma'an tried to get rid of the child-man-djinn, Your Honour. She called it 'creature' so as to degrade it, hoping against hope that the dishonouring would make Zümrüt resign. When he did not give in, she turned on her side and slept. When she slept, he slept. When she ate, he ate, and soon the granddaughter of Ma'an stopped being scared and bothered. True to his promise, Zümrüt was a sweet and obedient companion. She got used to him the way you get used to your shadow.

The granddaughter of Ma'an and Zümrüt continued on her unpredictable travels. A few times, thanks to the ingenuity of the djinn, she dodged thugs and dubious men. Tired, but safe and sound, she reached the hill and knew the house to go to: the one with Fatima's hand on the knob and the ivy climbing up its chapped blue paint. The door with the two different numbers – 1:3 and 5:8 – contending for acknowledgement, just the way her father had described it to her.

She told the old man who opened the door that the alchemist Ma'anoğlu had sent her. Upon hearing the name the Sheikh welcomed the guest like she bore the imperial stamp. She asked to use the bathroom and returned from it a full-fledged girl. The Sheikh was not surprised by the change in appearance; appearances are ephemeral to believers.

Even though the Sheikh could not see Zümrüt, one of the things he most liked in the granddaughter of Ma'an was the space she left behind and all around herself as if she felt the air was filled with spirits and wanted to pay them courtesy, or as if she wanted to occupy the least possible amount of space lest others want to expand and loiter. The politeness implicit in her behaviour made the Sheikh trust the girl, as he had trusted her father. Once upon a time the Druze had protected the Kurds from the infidel Crusaders too, back on Mount Lebanon.

The granddaughter of Ma'an and her adopted uncle the Sheikh began to conduct their experiments. The girl taught the Sheikh all the practical knowledge that had been passed down to her, and the Sheikh told her what these things meant in theory. 4, 9, 2, 3, 5, 7, 8, 1, 6 made the magic square. Sulphur and Mercury produced gold, but only when the five observable planets were in the right order, and only when the sun itself was the perfect distance from the earth. They studied and taught each other until one evening – and again a stormy and rainy one at that – they heard a feeble knock on the door, like that of a tired traveller.

When the Sheikh opened the door on that rainy night, he saw two men before him, one with a moustache newly forming, the other not yet old and very small. They introduced themselves as travelling historians. The young one said he was an Orphan, and that's how they began referring to him, and the older man said, 'He calls me Little Father and I quite like it.'

About a Door

Srdjan Srdic

I could write a word or two about that little one, and how he stands before a door. It was Saturday, going on for six, the little one had arrived and stood there, nothing else was happening. I don't know who could find this significant and what might be written about nothing. The little one was nondescript, but such was the time as well, history found itself in a rift, sizzling with all kinds of follies. Many stand before many a door, there is nothing new or special to it, people and doors have been written about: it is not an exceptional topic. I am rather well informed about that kid. Twenty years have elapsed since then, I am not certain, however, that time matters much. Time both passes and does not pass, both exists and does not exist. The same is true of that little one, there, he exists anew, exactly as he used to be, whether it is twenty years or less is all the same. Whether it is he himself makes no difference, since I see what I see. People believe what they want to believe, not that they are desirous of other things beyond measure. They can trust me too, nothing will change if they do, I will recount what I wish. Let them do whatever they want with it. There is paper and there is fire and that is all there is. The little one slept in a big room. The thing with the door happened in spring, which is fair to mention, so as not to look down on the kid with unnecessary pity, because it wasn't cold in the room that morning, but it was gloomy, the boy could still make out: a bed, another bed and yet another one, a table, a wardrobe, a mirror. Noteworthy objects and their silhouettes. The longer you are in the dark, the better you are at discerning things, which is no trifling advantage. The little one found it hard to get up before five, which he never came to terms with, it would be right to remark that there is something evil and sadistic in the voices you hear at that time, the voices that have to tell you this and that. I wouldn't say that the number of those who would listen at that time is too large, nor is the number of those who would listen at all too large, but there are stories and that is it, nothing can ever change the fact of the story, because there is no interest to it, none whatsoever. No one expects anything from a story, no one wise. Some voices were heard from the dark, which was a usual occurrence, otherwise the little one wouldn't get up, someone had to do that for him, the people from that house are dead today, and probably it is the same case with the house, and it is painful to remember all those dead people from the dead house after the numerous years, perhaps twenty, perhaps less. The rest is a lie, long-term memory distorts, and what remains is not even semblance, it is other than what it used to be, a story that is not important, for if it were important, people wouldn't die, neither would houses die. Since everything is equally significant and insignificant, even the kid before the door is equally a story, whatever opinion one would have of it. It is possible to tell billions of stories about that little one, there were things there, but he himself would opt for a few, if he had to make any choice, because beyond the chosen stories lies calculated sense, and there is hope of the existence of calculated sense, and the hope arouses thought about stories as messages to be deciphered before it's too late, as if anyone would benefit from them. The trouble with the story about the door lies in the fact that nothing happened, and the sooner we all acknowledge this, the sooner we will give up story-telling illusions. The little one stood there, the world also stood, and this lasted a while, an image of this has remained, which is a story, and all this is about that image/story. The story about the door is an apology of any conceivable stasis, if it has to be anything at all. Even today at that very place is the door, the river, the small bridge, the electro-technical school, the high school, the court, the Youth Club, the museum, the access roads, the red kiosks, the bike racks, the whole lot is still there. River, concrete and lawns. Children from the school buildings run along the river, until it turns too cold to run. Some of them run, others look at them calling out remarks, all this around the river is rather intensive. On this particular morning I would write about, no one was there. It was different in winter, prisoners were brought out to clean the snow from the bridge, monitored by guards armed with automatic guns. They reached the town market later on (if I am not mistaken, the market is no longer where it used to be, but I couldn't swear to it) and kept on cleaning, as the village vendors who came to work first insulted them, shouting: 'Boo convicts, boo bandits, it serves you right, fiends!' Hard-working folk they are, with a proverbially high opinion of themselves, those vendors working in such a manner. Again, no one thinks the best of the river, although it has no smell that wouldn't be in direct relation to people and their affairs, the crowd, however, passes by and swears at the river with a common aside to the effect that only a couple of other places have a similar odor: the dog pound and the starch factory. So, the little one heard one of those voices, once alive, and he followed it. Old age suffused the adjacent room, he passed through it sullenly, in the bathroom he washed and partially roused, he washed his hands with a bar of yellow children's soap (only such soap was used in that house, until it disappeared [which is good for the principle of association]) and he squeezed the Kolynos toothpaste onto his brush (only such toothpaste was used in that house, until it disappeared [which is also very good]). He rinsed his mouth, returned to the kitchen, sat down and leant on the table, tea with indistinctly sweetish taste was already there, and next to the full mug scrambled eggs were steaming, looking appetizing, but the little one didn't feel like breakfast, he had about ten minutes to do so many things, rushing about exhausted and perturbed him in terms of feasibility and ultimate effect. That's why he did this: he sprinkled half the contents of the saltshaker onto the plate with the scrambled eggs, rose and went back to the dark room where he got dressed in no time, it sometimes so happened that he slept the night in the clothes he'd worn the previous day, but this was not such a night, as the morning was not as any other, at least he always thought there was something extraordinary in that, there, before the door. Behind the door was supposed to be music, and this is what he hoped for when he first arrived in this town, it was supposed to be the town of music, unlike the town in which he was born and raised, where there was no music, there was no such music, there was not enough music, this is why he cherished hopes that he would find music in a new town, but it isn't always easy with hopes. He had arrived and for months now he'd been struggling to convince himself that he was not mistaken, that music was everywhere, that that was the right music, but this wasn't the case, music was elsewhere, in different places and with different people, behind the door some people squirmed, he got to know them, shortly afterwards his interest in most of them waned, and a similar fate befell the fake town of music, or the town of fake music. Some sort of music was heard there and music experts ascended the stairs clutching printed notes in their hands, obedient students following in their wake, thinking they would acquire the privileges of music, which was not happening, and there were also those apathetic when it came to music, most often they didn't feel like anything, so they morosely observed the world out of the music cage. Of all disappointments, and their sum total is certainly not small, which a random objective calculation will show, the greatest is disappointment in music, when it occurs, and when it actually occurs, one stays in a noisy, deafened space, which is a paradox, but a true paradox, and against this paradox one can do nothing whatsoever. The little one stood before a mirror, it was unlike later before the door, on the other side of the door there could easily be nothing, whereas with the mirror it was completely different, this is why he liked to stand before the mirror, in winter, in the afternoon, it was dark outside, and in the depth of the mirror it wasn't dark, which delighted and encouraged him. He looked at the clock, it was a solid Soviet clock, a present from a man now dead, the time was approaching, he took the box with his instrument and started on his way. The voices greeted him cordially, their owners were alive at the time, and there seemed to be no surprises to brace oneself for. However, the knowledge of the fake music in the fake town of music was indeed a surprise to get prepared for, but who would know this, so now it was necessary to suffer in the school of music, and such boys never suffer, they resist and think they have all possible rights and that they are isolated from the craved outcomes which they await in secret, in no time at all they turn into revolt per se, raving and confronting the illogical construction they qualify as the system, and they do so in order to pay knightly deference to the object of their own animosity. The little one shut the gate behind him and went on to catch the train, trains have an advantage over people, they are indifferent towards the urges of leaving, coming and arriving, there were not many trains back then, only a few would steal out of the historical rift, and the little one had to wake up before five so as to successfully catch one of the rare trains and get there in time for the Saturday orchestra rehearsal, because, for all the lies about music, he was dedicated to the duty the music suggested, and he didn't want to betray it, as it was gradually betraying him, turning its back on him mercilessly. To be better than music, it was a strong argument when it came to the showdown of self-reconsideration. He comprehended this a month before the event at the door, he kept trying to play a modern French composition, a vibrant solo de concours, he wasn't even close to success, but he sensed he knew what it was supposed to be like, and that on the other side there were those who sounded successful but felt nothing, he was brimming with this intuitive achievement, shut inside a sterile classroom for individual instrumental instruction, upstairs, on the second floor, the left wing of the corridor, he lifted a window shutter and spotted kayakers pushing hard away down the river in their elongated vessels, elegant, powerful and handsome. It was worthwhile sticking it out until the end of March, everything was to change then, and it was possible to avoid the waiting room, up until then it was cold, those who waited smoked, wrapping in newspaper sheets something that wasn't regular tobacco, playing cards, worn Hungarian cards showering across laid pigskin bags. As soon as the first April days came, passengers waited for trains sprawling on the station platform, the boy occupied a place on the corroded railing remains, and out of habit I kept turning my head in the north direction, where the railway signal was changed, announcing the arrival of a train. A man's day was born out of hubbub, the boy reasoned, squeezed between workers villagers passengers, overhearing the tongues rattling against the palates and filling-studded cavities, it seemed to him that he was invisible, and the invisibility was good, like the mild sun on the neighboring fields. The rhythm of the train like morphine and like blue-green and like steam from sometime machines for paving periphery crossroads. The boy tried not to lose his footing as a reflex action, he didn't need to, he couldn't fall, because he didn't have where to fall, people cancelled the laws of physics, you couldn't leave and get to a place where there wasn't a human language, because you thought in a human language which was hopeless, but without which you couldn't even be hopeless, you couldn't be anything, I knew that, even then I knew. And there was a piano: a badly tuned piano, a classroom on the ground floor, and there the little one made it his habit to pursue his search for forcefully interrupted dreams, the piano was man's friend, for it sounded without too much invested effort, touch was all that was needed, tone was touch, there was no question there about the quality of tone as aesthetically decisive, the quality of touch, the touch drawn in the eardrum. The kid would do this when he was early, he would enter the classroom, remove the lid from the piano and touch it, nothing else, because you could do nothing else if you wanted your dreams back, the plan would have to look exactly like this. And the train was slow and it was slowing down, the suburbs, tilting hangars, industrial landscapes for accustomed observers, nine kilometers in linguistic secretions, nine kilometers to the fake town of fake music, times nine in return and nine the next day and the day after, perhaps not on Sundays and perhaps not on some other days. I longed for air. The door was opened, the train was in motion, despite the metal warning signs, no one paid heed, Moses was anachronism, those in the front jumped out chased by the mania of urgency, deftly, skillfully, landing on their feet and going on towards hospitals, markets and smoky, distant contours. The little one extricated himself so as not to be seen, even though no one noticed him, who cared, and the little one crept in between the freight wagons, jumping over their couplings by means of safety handles, it smelt of coal and serious poverty. When he crossed over (he duly paused and glanced left and right, although there were no trains at all) I started over the embankment, there were other ways as well, even better ones, but he chose this one, and he stuck to it, since even then the little one's character was unwavering, conservative in decisions he held for a certain reason to be correct, an unfaltering, fanatically and stubbornly consistent type. The absence of people and sounds started right after passing the embankment, I cannot say I noticed it immediately, it could easily be a projection caused by the time distance and the wish to write the effects that were actually missing, but that determine the story structurally (and semantically, inevitably). Still, in the maze of streets down which he had to plunge in order to reach the school, the little one passed the university, a butcher's, he liked to loiter in front of butcher shops and count the pieces of bacon on hooks and piled sausages, he passed by a pub where students of mechanical engineering studied, and by a dark house entwined in ivy, in that house and its damp, depressive yard he would find a student of Italian and her elder sister, he would spend an afternoon with them, they would laugh, he would leave and not forget all that, this would happen three years after the day I am writing about, I recall it clearly, but I can by no means gather why I recall it, of all the things I could have memorized, why this of all and what it means, when you remember it and recount it on. Then, the prison walls, it was once known, the prison was where the court was, there was no transport of those on whose minds was escape, fustiness, lichen, and countless stories about what went on behind the walls, the little one had an inkling of it, of the solitary confinement cell, of the attic and the basement, the Sunday soup of prison pigeons, two Hungarian watchmen and an insane colossus of a guard, who insisted on working night shifts, so as to welcome ruffians, rapists and irate alcoholics eagerly, and beat them bloodthirstily without witnesses, investigators and record-keepers. When one stands opposite the court façade, the school seems to be in a luminous depression, surrounded on all sides by buildings taller and more monumental, shadowy and stately: the school looks as if it had sunk into something, slipped into all those melodies buried in its history. Viewed from the bridge this depression is even more pronounced, and the little one wondered whether the real secret, what was painfully difficult to fathom, was in the depths of the river, rather than behind the door of such an insignificant and worthless building. From that very bridge, which is merely a strictly functional steel monster, descend some steps, the little one went that way, and I heard my own steps, it was Saturday, and it was early, and it was the first time I'd heard anything in that noisy, deafened space, on the paved path leading up to the semicircular concourse in front of the door. I walked on leisurely, and a flash of the only just risen sun leant on my shoulders, crisscrossing the cold school façade, as if only then did the little one become wide awake, he raised his head and stopped, at first almost bumping into the door decorated with tall, iron figures. I know no one who has heard the sun, or colors, or smells, or shadows, but I can confirm that all this could be heard then, there, there was nothing else, the little one kept spinning in wonder, searching for the place where all this was coming from, but there was nothing, and in the nothing was heard the sun, and melodic colors, and shadows. The boy took another half-step and touched the door, which usually opened easily, I'd done that so many times, but nothing happened this time, one couldn't go any further, and I stayed there, before the door, alone, many people consider possibilities, this is one of the possibilities, solitude, absolute solitude, it is also a possibility, but as a theory, as a draft or a logical resultant, because there appears perplexity, one wonders: how to know who I am if there is no one else, and there was no one else there, someone had locked the door and forgot about it, someone who didn't expect that anyone like me existed. What else could anyone be but a totality of relations, whereas there, before the door, there was no such intimacy, I stood in a membrane that had suppressed the world, swelling with light, not heat, not winter light, but only light, only from the effect which shaped scenes and spaces and without which there was not even that trifling nothing with which I was left before the door. The second time I almost thrust at the door, disconsolate, not because I looked forward to what was behind, but because absolute solitude was equal to absolute deafness, I muttered a chain of meaningful syllables and they didn't find adequate sense, because they were addressed to no one, and they couldn't be addressed to me, because I was nothing, like all that piled stone around, lawns and indifferent trees, syllables and words ceased on the inside of the membrane, bursting, fragmentizing, vanishing. So I stood before the door, I could go back, towards the safe place where I'd come from, to search for trains and their tracks, wherever they led, wagons and embankments, to recall, that above all else, but I didn't recall anything, and then there was nothing, when you could recall nothing and no one, there was no movement and no way back, towards the trains and tracks. The boy standing still, the door standing still, the world standing still, and they in it, the world-membrane which everyone had forgotten and which had forgotten to inhabit itself with concepts, notions and beings, I found myself there, with my instrument, my useless instrument, a whistle that did not announce itself in tone, since tone was duration, vibration in time, and time had cancelled itself, annulled itself, for me to stay there all by myself before that door, all on my own, man was seldom less than that. And I cannot say that it lasted, because it didn't last, and it did last, if it hadn't lasted, I couldn't recall it, and I couldn't invent it and write it down, the boy stood, not anticipating anything about the man writing about the boy who didn't know anything about him, but he knew that there was a door through which you couldn't pass, and you were made to stand and wait for another man to write another door, the one through which people and boys passed, covering the same different ways, you waited for a man with right words, with passwords and codes for people, boys, women, girls, alive as well as the dead, what was what wasn't what could have been and what would never never never be. The sun behind the back, the river. Paper, fire, and everything there is.

Sleeper

Lesley Glaister

To avoid the cramped intimacy that the sleeper cabin would afford, she got ready for bed in the Ladies' at King's Cross. She brushed her teeth and spat furtively into the basin before splashing her face and angling it into the dryer's roar. Odd to be getting ready for bed there, but she wasn't the only one. A young woman, stripped to the waist to display pierced nipples, was uninhibitedly lathering her armpits. Jan smiled across the ranks of basins at her, but she was locked, scowlingly into her own ablutions. In a cubicle, Jan changed from dress and pointy shoes into leggings, long T-shirt and Crocs – a beddish outfit, suitable also for a yoga class. Without the insistent clutch of her bra, her breasts slumped and her body readied itself for sleep.

Max was waiting on the concourse outside the Gents', a fleck of toothpaste caught in the corner of his mouth. Jan smiled; pointed to the place on her own lip and he rubbed it off. *Intimacy*, she noticed with a flutter of alarm, the sort of thing that couples do. It was approaching midnight. WH Smiths, and most of the other outlets were shut, but there was a Coffee Inc with a queue. Jan found a bench and waited while Max went to buy hot chocolate for them both. She'd had too much wine, and wanted nothing more than to shut her eyes. Tired people with purgatorial faces dragged cases round, and a crowd of women, wearing horns and tails, squawked and shrieked.

In the queue, Max looked short and ordinary. When she'd met him six weeks ago Jan had thought he looked like a grocer or a bank-clerk, or maybe a geography teacher – and he did, in fact, teach IT skills. He was not the type she usually went for, but she'd been captivated by his GSOH – not that he'd even mentioned it himself.

'Hmmm,' Trish had said, looking over her shoulder at the screen to see the thinning hair and gormless rictus with which he'd chosen to advertise himself.

'No,' Jan agreed, 'he's not exactly...'

But in his profile he claimed to be boring, flatulent and scrofulous, which made her laugh. Another problem was his height – his profile claimed that he was 5ft 7in and she'd really been in the market for 5ft 10in upwards. Even 5ft 7in turned out to be something of an exaggeration, but he'd turned up for their first date with a tape measure and a signed confession, so how could she hold two inches against him? He was still a smidge taller than she was if she wore flat shoes and hunched a bit.

Some of the hen party women were in the queue behind him, towering and flirting. She saw him turn and smile up at something one of them said. She caught a policeman yawning and she caught the yawn, hand over her hollowed mouth as she watched tomorrow's papers being wheeled across the concourse.

Max returned with the chocolate, and sat beside her. 'Sleepy?' he said.

She nodded and took the tall, hot, paper cup.

'Someone's a bit the worse for wear.' He nodded over at one the drunken women stumbling on her stilettos. 'Ever been to a hen do?'

'My sister's,' she said. 'But it wasn't like this.'

Trish's had been cocktails in a local bar and then a club, actually very tame. Much of the conversation had revolved round husbands and children, and most of them had gone home by 1 am leaving Trish and Jan to keep the side up. Jan's shoes had been too tight and she'd been sleepy, but they had to stay till at least 2, she'd told herself, sneaking a look at her watch. She'd brought them each a Daiquiri, and they'd settled into seats at the bar.

'It'll be you next,' had been Trish's inevitable comment.

The cocktail stick in Jan's glass poked up her nostril.

'You think?' she'd said.

This was her sixth date with Max – and, she'd decided, the last.

'But why?' Trish had said this morning on the phone. 'I thought it was going so well. What's wrong with him?'

'I don't know why *you* need *me* to be with someone,' Jan said.

'What?'

'Nothing.'

'What *is* wrong with him then?'

The trouble was, nothing was actually wrong with him. Usually, on a first date there's an immediate get-out clause: slip-on shoes; meaty ears; a grating voice. Or else, a little further into the evening, a naff joke; incompatible opinions or a whiff. But with Max, though there was certainly no wow factor, neither was there anything to complain about. He looked considerably better than his photograph. His eyes were pale brown, grainy like scuffed leather, rather earnest. He made her think old-fashioned words like earnest, kind, sincere. He wore unobjectionable clothes and footwear, his ears were pale and flat against his head, there was no dandruff or beer-gut and his voice was pleasant.

'We'll be boarding soon,' he said, looking at his watch.

'Looking forward to my bed,' she said. She'd booked them onto the sleeper back to Edinburgh – though he'd been in favour of a hotel. But having already decided that this was their last date, she'd told him she had to be back for work in the morning. The sleeper would be perfect for an amicable break up: nice little bunks, too small for intimacy but still chummy. (That word alone would have turned her right off if he'd said it.)

She'd planned to tell him earlier, but it was hard to gauge the right moment. On the way down would have spoiled the whole trip; before dinner might have ruined their appetites; during the party would have been too much of a dampener of the spirits. Maybe now was the moment? Just spit it out – but when she turned to speak she saw that he was smiling at a tired child trailing after its drunk and bickering parents.

'Poor wee mite,' he said and did something with his face that made the child smile. Seeing, the father scowled at Max, grabbed the child and yanked it away.

Instead of *This isn't working for me*. 'Wanker,' came supportively from her lips.

Max had paid extra for cream and marshmallows and she took a sweet, chewy mouthful. He gave a gaping yawn, and instead of turning away she searched eagerly for a bad tooth or lumpy tongue – but it all looked fine in there. Full marks for dental health as well as mental. She sighed.

Even in bed, which they'd only done twice the flaw was not apparent. He knew his anatomy, was neither melodramatically passionate nor mechanical, and seemed genuinely appreciative of her (admittedly fairly average) charms. His skin smelled wholesome and his body was firm and nicely furred in all the right places.

When their platform was announced, they discarded their paper cups and followed the soporifically trudging crowd to the sleeper. Carriage H turned out not to be a cabin with chummy bunks, but an ordinary carriage crammed with couchettes – and almost filled by the hen party, still in mid celebration.

'Oh fuck,' Jan said.

'Let's see.' He took and examined the tickets. 'This is right,' he said. 'I thought you said you'd booked –'

'I thought I'd booked a cabin,' she said, squaring up for a row. This would be it then, he'd reveal a nasty temper, and there would be her reason. *He's got a terrible mouth on him*, she'd tell Trish, *it was an honest mistake but you should have heard him*! Her eyes scanned the carriage: unfortunately there was no scope for storming off. She waited, bristling, for his ire, but he just grinned and shrugged.

'Oh well,' he said, 'at least it's cosy.'

Cosy was the sort of word that could put you off a person.

'Let me put your bag up.'

'I can do it.'

There were folded eye-masks and menus waiting on their couchettes.

'What do you think of Hugh then?' Max asked. They had travelled down from Edinburgh to London for his brother's 40th birthday party.

'He's a laugh,' she said. 'Not like you at all. I mean physically – not that you're not a laugh.'

He twinkled at her. That was the only word to describe what happened in his eyes. What happens when a person twinkles? Is it a physical process? Not everyone can twinkle, that's for sure. Her first thought on being introduced to Hugh had been, shame you're not your brother. A shabby thought. Now he was possessed of the wow factor. Hugh was tall; Hugh was broad-shouldered; long-lashed; splendidly suited and booted. His dark hair curled onto his collar, his eyes were blue, his lashes ridiculous, his voice had a deep, sexy scrape. She wriggled in her couchette at the thought of him.

'Impressive, eh?' Max said.

She shrugged. 'If you like that sort of thing.'

Max looked at the dark window and she watched the unflattering reflection of his expression as he spoke. 'I know you shouldn't hold being good-looking and good at everything against someone.' He let out a bitter rag of laughter. 'He did better at school, good at sports, got all the best girls, he can even fucking *sing*.'

Jan relaxed. This was it then, this was the flaw – envy is a most unattractive trait. And *all the best girls* indeed!

A balloon, red and shiny with black horns and the words, You Wee Devil, floated down and biffed him in the face. He did a header and grinned. 'I'm a green eyed monster,' he said and shrugged. Behind them a cork popped and hit the roof, eliciting squeals of laughter and *Do you mind keeping it down,* from someone further back. One of the devils swayed past, mumbling, 'I'm busting for a piss.'

'God, we'll never get to sleep,' Jan grumbled. She took the eye-mask from its wrapper. 'I'm going to shut my eyes for a bit.' He patted her knee and left his hand there. The mask was tight around her head. As soon as she had it on she felt ridiculous, but committed to a temporary blindness.

'You're so fussy,' Trish had said this morning.

'I'm not.' Jan had pictured Trish's Barry and bitten back the obvious retort. 'There's just not the chemistry,' she'd said, imagining how under-whelmed her friends would be if introduced to Max.

'Chemistry!' Trish had tutted. 'Chemistry's a myth. I sometimes wonder if you really *want* to find someone.'

Behind them there was a further shriek and buzz as the bride-to-be opened an electrical gift.

'Call the guard,' demanded the grumpy voice from further back.

'Sodom and Gomorrah,' said someone else.'What is the world coming to?'

Bzzz-zzz-zzz went the item and a woman gave a mock climactic shriek.

Max snorted. Jan pulled off the eye-mask, just in time to see him pop his contact lenses into his palm and stow them into a little case. She noticed weary mauve scoops under his eyes.

'What did you mean: *all the best girls*?' she said.

He did his twinkle again. 'Then I meant, when we were kids. If I ever took a girl home, she only had to take one look at him ...'

She thought of Hugh's long shanked wife, with her sheaves of glassy hair, and looked down at her own plumply legginged thighs. This was the moment.

'So you think Shania is better than me?' she said. 'You're calling me second rate?'

He hesitated a beat too long before he shook his head. She looked at him with a show of disbelief before snapping the eye-mask back on and shrinking her thigh eloquently away from his. How *dare* he think that, she thought, attempting to whip herself into a frenzy of rage, though she knew what he meant and, in fact, agreed entirely.

'I'm going to sleep,' she announced. *Second rate!* Wait till she told Trish that! *Second rate* – although it was her phrase not his. But no one could be expected to conduct a relationship with someone who implied that about them.

Outside the dark country flowed past behind the windows though there was nothing to see but reflections, and inside the eye-mask nothing but smudged memories and an irritating pressure on her lashes. She lifted a corner of the eye-mask and peeped at Max. He was reading his novel and smiling.

Later she woke, surprised to have been able to sleep. It will be easy, she thought, at the station I'll just say, *This isn't working.* That's the accepted code: *this isn't working out for me.* She pulled her eye-mask up to look at him. He, unmasked, was asleep, head lolling, a trail of drool hanging from his chin. His hands were loose and open on his thighs. Stubble, some of it grey, made him look grubby and ageing. His eye-lids were veined like leaves and through them she saw the slide and flicker of his eyeballs. Dreaming, she thought, and swallowed against the sudden threat of tears. A whole world was going on in there, a whole wide world of dreams. His hands lay loose and vulnerably open in his lap.

She put one finger out to stroke his palm, and in his sleep, he grasped it.

Dog Trouble

Anna Stewart

Woman's head found in plastic bag; teenager sets fire to innocent bystander; lassie sucks disabled man's eyeball out wi vacuum cleaner; you see it in all the news.

But I'd rather look out this window than at that daft screen, take that telly away, what do I want to watch all that drivel for?

Nobody looks out their windows anymore, they don't know what's going on, we don't look out for each other like we used to. But you're born alone, you die alone, that's what I keep telling myself.

Take November, there was a lassie out there in the dark, dragging her foot along that road and nobody watching.

But me, I gets my specs on and have a look, see what's happening.

The wind was lashing up a right spray from the sea, and there she was, hurrying along in them big daft heels and that skimpy wee dress. I could see her foot was giving her jip, I know pain when I see it, and she kept turning round so I thought she mustae been running from something.

I thought, ach, it'll be a man, and if I'd been any younger I mighto gone out there to give him what for, I've never take any rubbish from men, they know not to bother me.

But I couldnae see a man, I couldnae see anything.

The road behind was all dark, just them waves pelting up from the sea and triangles o rain falling sidey-ways in they street lamps.

Everything went quiet for a second and the lassie stopped and turned, kindo stiff.

Then came this tapping, like one o them military drums, pounding, all sticks onto skin, or teeth onto wood; rattling, a kindo rattling sound.

Then I saw twa shiny circles, moving fast in the dark wi the noise.

They got closer and I could see they were eyes, bobbing up and down wi' some body close to the ground, bouncing flecks o blue-black muscle in and out the lamps; a dog, a great big dog, hammering its nails into the tarmacadam, chasing.

I didnae know how it could be off its leash rampaging down the street like that, maniac o an animal so it was, chewing air like full o rabies, wi giant streams o spit pouring out its mouth, then flinging back, hitting it in the face.

She was dragging her foot too slow, *run, run, run*, for she was far enough away, *run now you daft lass, run*.

She moved faster across the road, forgetting her pain, and heading in my direction.

The dog spotted her and followed.

I shut my light off so they couldnae see me watching.

I could see the dog better then, wi its ribcage bounding, swallowing its head so it landed closer. No animal, just bits o fur-lined bone wi air moving about inside.

She was running towards my window, looking through my nets right at uz. I was relieved for a second coz she kept running past, but then I heard her going down the alley, round the backs.

I moved as quick as I could to the back door, but it takes some time in my condition, and my chair always sticks in that alcove through the kitchen.

When I got there, the door was near off its hinges wi all the pounding going on outside, she was banging that hard wi her fist and saying,

'Let uz in Missus! Let uz in!'

I was affy glad I'd put the bolt on.

I heard the dog barking, and the girl slump down, then in my letterbox she whispered,

'Let uz in Missus, that dog's efter uz.'

But I thought naw, I cannie let her in coz she'll be bringing that dog, and I've enough to worry about.

So I kept quiet and hoped she'd go away.

But she didnae go away, she stayed outside greetin against my door coz she knew that dog would find her.

I heard it coming in my front garden so I knew it wouldn't be long coming round the back.

I wheeled in closer and said, 'Mibbee it's yir perfume'

She said, 'Eh?'

I said again, a wee bitty louder so she'd hear through the wood, 'Mibbee the dog doesnae like yir perfume.'

She never said anything after that, but she mustae knew I couldn't let her in, no the way things were in here.

And besides, that bolt on the back door's affy stiff.

I heard her getting up but I couldnae really see her through the back window, it's that wee bit high for me, I just saw the top o her head for a second, but then it disappeared.

There was a noise like she was moving something, a scraping kindo sound and I thought aye, she'll be picking up one o them boulders, the nice painted ones that my Jeannie got me from Homebase. I shouted out to her, 'Dinnae you be stealing stuff from my garden.'

And she said, 'Shut yir face yi stupid auld bitch.'

Then I hoped the dog would get her.

I heard her going down the alley again, so I headed back to the living room, getting stuck in the alcove on the way.

The dog was growling and I thought, oh aye it mustae seen her now. It started barking, right hard, and there was some shifting about.

She wasn't making any noise, I thought that was strange. But the dog was barking louder.

Then I heard a thud, kindo skull on skull like a coupla bairns banging heads, and the barking stopped. There was another thud, and the dog started whining... another and the whining stopped.

There were a good few thuds after that, but I thought they were just for good measure, then something crashed and made the floor shake, and her daft heels went clip-clopping down the alley.

I saw her from the living room window, hobbling away, half-dressed in all that rain.

I thought about going out the front door and having a wee look but it's an affy fankle getting up and down that ramp, and I was a bit scared the dog might still be living, even though I knew deep down he couldnae be.

The lights went on in the house next door, and things started to seem more normal. I looked down at my hands and saw they were shaking, and I thought it'd be good to phone Jeannie, but I knew she'd only get annoyed.

About half-an-hour passed and a police car drove up outside my house, there was twa o them, a man and a woman. They went and rung the bell on the house next door, and I could see my neighbour Mr. Horn talking to them and pointing down the alley to my back garden.

Then the twa police and Mr. Horn all started nosying round on my property without even asking.

When Mr. Horn went back in his house, the police came and rung on my door. They were both soaking wet and I didn't let them in coz I didn't want them dragging their feet on my carpet.

They asked if I'd seen anything going on, and I just told them, 'Aye, a lassie's killed a dog out there, and she came in my back garden and stole one o my ornamental boulders from Homebase to do it.'

They asked if I'd seen the dog and I said, 'Aye, it was affy lively.'

The policewoman said, 'Well it's no very lively anymore' and she looked affy upset about it, like she might greet.

I said, 'What's it like?'

She said it was a right mess and I wouldn't want to see it, but I thought how does she know I wouldn't want to see it? I might've, I've eyes in my head.

By the time I got out there to have a wee look, they'd gone and got someone to clear it all up.

They asked if I was willing to be a witness and I said, 'Aye, put me down for that.'

The policewoman said she'd come round and see uz in the morning to get a full statement, but I said to wait for afternoon. I didn't tell her why, but there's a wifey that comes in the mornings from the council, no that I'm needing her, it's Jeannie's doing.

That night I had this dream where the dog was chasing uz, I moved right quick in it, coz I was a lass again and my legs seemed to work affy good. But when I looked down I saw loadsae woodworm in my bones, boring wee holes, crumbling bits o leg off.

When the policewoman came the next day she said I must be tired after all that fright, but I said nah, it didn't faze me.

I asked her if she wanted a cup o tea and she took one, I gave her a coupla them mint Viscount biscuits, but thinking on it now, they mightae been stale.

She was right nosey and came in my kitchen and was looking in my cupboards when I was getting the tea out. She said I didn't have much in there, and asked if I was looking after myself, but I told her I'm no a big eater.

She said she had twa bairns, wee boys, and asked if I'd any myself. So I told her about my Jeannie, and that she lives down the Borders. She said it was a shame she lives so far away, but I said sometimes mothers and daughters dinnae get on, and she's lucky she's got sons.

After that I found out all sorts. She said that girl was on drugs, some new one. They picked her up outside the arcade a coupla hours after they'd been at mine. She was all rigid and that, just standing against the wall, no moving. Anyhow she'd been at some party and they'd given drugs to that dog, and it'd gone mad and went for her.

Ended up I had to go to court and everything.

That girl, she got three months in a young offenders for killing the dog. And fined for breaking and entering my property, causing vandalism o my boulder, and smashing some o my patio when she dropped it. I'll get five hundred pounds compensation for all that.

Lately though I've been getting these weird phone calls from folk I dinnae ken, I'm wondering if it's something to do wi her. There was a couple o eggs thrown at my window an all the other day; lads on bikes.

Couldae been her brothers.

Midrash

Mark Buckland

The man in the gorilla suit jumped from the wardrobe, reeling shoppers panic. That skit was met by a brass of laughter from the row behind me, a cathartic laugh, one that says that with every dip and rock of the plane's wings, you know the last thing you'd see is a gorilla with a man's head, chuckling and directing the innocent pranked's view to a nearby camera. Humour that barters funny for universal appeal, some Canadian slapstick unmemorable other than it might be the last thing you see before you find death by turbulence. And the Scandinavians love it.

He doesn't love it. His head is in Proust, pretending to read. His boiling denim legs crushed by the seat in front, twigstick fingers humming at the pages.

I have to write a piece on ChangeCube.

What's that?

You know, the cube game people. The kids' game.

You have to go there?

Yeah. Your home town, right.

Not his home town, not a generation back, not with that cartoon Arab stubble; blue eyes that betray the dark huddle of features. Not dad's home town, the north.

Let's go together. I'll ask my parents for the summer house.

Summer house, this started it all. We have to change the dates, get new flights he'd said, as if you can just get flight dough from nowhere. He's wealth; restrictions, reductions confuse him.

He crosses yet another uncomfortable leg and preens to me.

We land soon.

Yeah.

You ok?

Sure, yeah. How's the book?

Interesting, he murmurs.

Interesting how?

He doesn't reply, because he hasn't read a word. Because he doesn't read books.

Around me, then, and when we reached the tarmac, then the slow stew of pine wood and glass in the terminal were English speakers, but I'm the only native. I stutter a thanks at customs, because I can't remember the word for it, because the guard doesn't flit an eyelid, because it's all so unremarkable to them, my language. We're in woodland freeways then, he's driving with Springsteen turned up loud, rental car echo, singing along and mollifing every vowel in a breaking wave tongue, used to caressing long o's and low cu's. At the hotel, he nosedived the bed, while I did my hair in the bathroom mirror. He turned on the TV, car chase on it, before it flash-frames static, then a channel about chopping wood and building fires, a whole channel of it, he explained.

I looked at him through the side of the mirror, still had his denim jacket on, a long stretch of pale, washed blue, perfectly still, like an empty fish counter. He slid a hand over his hair and stared when it recoiled, enough jetlag slick to coat an Alaskan beach. You can imagine seals fucking drowning in the tide that his hair produces.

Let's go out tonight, yes?

I dunno, I gotta be over to the place in, like, two hours.

But it's early.

Yeah, but I'm tired.

I folded a hand around my waist. I imagined how it would look bigger, the skin stretched out to a globe, then I pushed my stomach in and saw myself 10lbs lighter. Thinner, better, more desired, better.

Yes, but, you see, like, everywhere is going to close early. It's Sunday. We don't eat late on the Sundays.

Ok.

Every Americanism he's ever heard coming into his voice, an accent unwelcoming to them, every piece of New York like a globalising ghost hanging around his mouth. Every word like you're being fellated by a McDonald's that's just opened in a nature reserve.

Will you be gone long?

Yes, I'll be long, I'm a journalist, my job takes a long time, longer than your job which is mostly collecting records and smoking. In a passing moment of idealism, yes, I'll be really long, like the rest of your life, long.

No. Like two hours max, yeah?

Yes, sure.

His phone chimed. He reached one long arm over the bed, without breaking his glacial pose and picks it up. He read. He frowned. I tied my hair back, I picked up my bag.

My parents are out of town.

I thought you said we'd meet them.

Yes, I thought so. But they have left town.

But they knew you were coming.

He flushed the air with a sigh, trying to huff the ceiling down.

Yes, they do that sometimes.

Like, how often are you back?

Too often.

Yeah, I gotta go, okay, we'll do something later, ok?

Yes, sure.

I went to kiss his forehead, but my hand just hung up in midair. Jerked move, end up looking like I'm shadowboxing. So I turned and left and moved outside, so I can pretend that I didn't hesitate.

I stand at the tram stop. There's a mother with her child in a pram. Blonde, blue eyed, quartz for teeth. She moves further down, to my other side when an African guy appears, his headphones making his neck juggle his head. There's an eternity of no-noise, I'm in the outskirts of the city, I can see the plains and the hills and a beating heart of stultifying silence.

Tram arrives and I get on, pram woman refuses help from me, African man doesn't see her and me. I get on and sit behind him. Hair knotted and skin on the back of his neck impetigo'd into an atlas. Pins a racoon finger against an earphone, maybe it's not working properly. He gets up and slides into the seats opposite me, facing me and stretches a limpet leg onto the pew opposite.

Tall, slack denim around his waist. I drift a hand over his belt buckle, lightly grazing it, brushing it down, before I slide two fingers down along a oil-spill beach black thigh, grabbing hold halfway down, squeezing the blood flow, to maim the vein. I drop to my knees, stripe the gold zipper on his flies, pop the top button. But lust is not a voyage. I can leave when they let me. Two more join the bus, little Spaldeen head old man and his wife, her hands like crepes, all slouching ridges and canals. My mother's hands never held that age. In January, the hands found a stillness, an idiosyncratic stillness, all of their own.

Next tram I get on, there's a little boy, staring at the plugs in my ears. I used to get that, I don't grow used to it. At *Vogue*, temping, strong word even for what it was, kibbling the coffee and pretending to write between paychecks. I got to be the girl with the plugs. Wasn't like I had them in there a long time, long enough that cycles of winter/summer fashion bled out into a pinkslip, before I bonneted over to a few other places. Crappy craft mags, 100 uses for a teacup, that thing, purpose for the white soul. Computing, that's something you could do; he was the first to say it, over the gaze of a stoop sat tallboy, one autumn night.

My father, the canuck, his daughter, the nerd. Gaming was now the name for it, which made it sound less innuendo and more just an upfront declaration of hobbying in collecting welfare checks and masturbating. The little boy laughs at me, he has his mother's eyes, blank away from me, he's swung over her shoulder. My father had two smiles, I only ever saw one. He'll be planning how to lie to me already, running hands over hotel bed sheets, heating cotton, creating the idea of another's departure, before he's even met her. I was doing this piece for this strutting lifestyle mag, middle of menopause gloss sheets, talking about dreams to kids, what's your favourite dream I asked this one kid, new to stateside, from India. The ones where I get to be the king, he said, honestly. The answer every man would give, most learn the theatre of hiding it for a while. He has. Not well, but he's versed.

He'll be back at the hotel, in the bar, just as I board a train. He'll be on a third cocktail, proselytizing one leg over a stool, prone, staring at the barmaid, speaking in a language I don't understand, all black marble and hard edges, bitten lips. Train leaves on time, precisely on the minute, a carriage of cool pattern baldness and shuffling briefcases. He'll be quiet at first, then there's that smile.

I never say my girlfriends, because that's the type of romcom stackwash you get to hearing around women in bars where we live, gumbas, clothes like beltways on their frames, so skeletal the cloth and skin never get to meet. I say my friends, even if my friends never say me. They pawn this one phrase around over yoga mats, over coffee, over a beer, trying out different ways it could be said, a reflexology of the words till they're bent out of shape, hardened, crooked.

I want him to stay with me.

The landscape becomes unstuck from the map, a blank, flat dish, pizza topping houses.

I want him to stay with me, they'll say. I'd never even thought. I came home one day to find one of the oldest memories had moved out, two years he'd hung there, leaving explanation and two receipts for Best Buy, a quart of mints and a gold key ring noosed around them, the Statue of Liberty from a warmer day, two 40oz down. They don't become significant, hurtful, till you picture his pockets outturned, drained of all mementos, consumable and permanent. A few still lived on the blocks around me; I get to be a spitoon, not sidewalk now.

I want him to stay with me, they'll say. As if every call he makes is a beckoning. You're in hock to this one, they say without lips. Train takes a long curve, melting through molehills now. After we're gone, it'll look beautiful in the snow.

The blonde hairs thin out, I'm the last one on the train. I get off at the last stop, to dim platform. The carriage ahead of me has been full, gaggles of unwashed teens, brown dreads, thick and flaxen. Employees.

ChangeCube is a city of Californian obelisks, glass and smooth edge. In the foyer, I see my reflection in the black marble desk as a woman slides me a visitors' pass. Clip to jacket. Wipe eyes. Ignore wrinkling cheeks.

He meets me, bald, imprisoned behind white, glassless spectacles. Shakes my hand, takes me over a long transparent corridor, suspended over thousands of computers, like lanterns at a refugee camp. A ping pong table at the end of the great hall. One of the players waves to us, two figures levitating above the workplace. He waves back.

He takes me into a conference room. One day, all interior designers who do conference rooms will meet, probably at a conference, and realise the unique, bold, innovative designs their clients demanded and they supplied are identical. Something will go bad in the Kool Aid at that meeting. He pops me on the desk like I weigh nothing, fumbles inside my shirt, handling my breasts, clutching between my legs, paws of a teenage in a drought. He says something like, didn't you bring any questions? And I stare at the water he's put down before me, no ice, not eco enough, the walls are bamboo, the glass recycled bottles, he explains, maybe he'll chastise me for my notepad not being made from hemp.

– What's the greatest achievement of ChangeCube?

He sighs. Could this have not been done over video call and variations on that phrase. It's more of a mood piece. It's more of an excuse for him to show me around where he grew up, where he can show me cool clubs he liked as a kid and ignore the swingsets and playparks he loved even before that, as if they were background tapestries. It's a piece that allows him to stand on detritus beaches, each smelted down with sewage, pope's hats, black bags and point at the mountains until we hope we develop longsightedness. It's a reason to endure your country, I smile. It'll be a mood piece. It'll be rewritten as clickbait, 50 gaming studios to see before you die, 5 reasons you must read about this Scandinavian hit game today, I'm still picking my jaw off the floor, one secret to a larger penis, fourteen Northern Europeans you won't believe exist. Read closely at line 34, listen closer at 0:54. He won't listen closely. He won't even read it.

He'll be drunk by now. He'll be in the room with the barmaid, barking at her, losing her name in a crowd of English and panting Scandavowels. If he hasn't scored with her, he'll have jacked off thirty or forty times, broken the seal on two minibar bottles before thinking that might be too far. Too far for an afternoon, not me.

He used to make me laugh. Dull barlight where I could hide my crooked teeth, I'd turn my laugh to the side and into my hands. I hope he will stay with me. What they mean is, I think he'll leave at any moment. We're in the elevator, minimal jazz like the sound of falling down stairs in the speakers, the whole place like a meat locker with more soul. It'll be a mood piece. The mood of imminent suicide, presented in an Ello profile.

He's showing me awards now, phallic bronzes, stiff pyramids, triumph. Spindled black letters that talk about beautiful products that change the world. You are the greatest deceit I ever met. You are the one memory that will imbed me like a stone. Kiddo, you are the great fugazi of boyfriends. We shake hands, I leave, I get on a train. I have a full notebook of notes that emerged from somewhere. The train has one girl opposite me, dead grass dreads in a summer dress. I dive between her legs, forking my tongue, she moans, reeling back, trying to climb out of her seat. He'll be asleep now, barmaid leaving the room, untugging her hair.

I reverse steps, descend stairs where I had once climbed, through carriage doors as a tape winding back, sit on the same benches. I am the unwinding wheel. By the time I reached the hotel, there is no threat of sunset. A man is outside the hotel, newspaper stand, hands in bubbled pockets. Front pages, Charlize Theron is behind tired sunglasses, pursued by letters, drop shadow English o's speared by lines. Newspapers carry pictures of black masks and dark flags. Forgotten deserts. I am alone in this experience. He is never alone, that's one of the true things about him.

The room is dark when I enter. He's in a halflight, curtains passed over windows. Still in the same position. There's ash on the bed, embers in a glass. Two candy wrappers contorting at his feet. TV still on.

I sit on the bed, softly.

How was it?

Fine. Y'know. Boring. Dull.

Hmm.

You alright?

Sure.

Your parents call you again?

No.

How can you watch TV this long?

Easily.

Back home, you watch TV this long, you'll see at least three gun crimes.

He smiles. First time in a generation, it will feel to him. I climb over, cling an arm to the flesh of the denim and his hand flops listless to my head, I am holding onto him, I am holding on, feeling down his ribs, asking him about tomorrow, my forehead palmed in his hand, summer house or not, maybe there's a boat trip, maybe we should go record collecting, what's the weather like at home, did you text my sister, I will forget my friend's phrase, their ideology, do you know they don't believe in watercoolers there, we'll laugh about that later and just smile for now, not eco, we are going to be okay, can we take your parents' boat out, you sailed alone as a kid, right, little boy alone, still alone on the waves, I didn't bring much cash, you know where's good to eat, because I will stay with him, I will stay with him.

Extract from the novel
Galloway: An Unreliable Tour

Hugh McMillan

A legendary painting, with its exact duplicate 'Midnight in Lerwick', it is one of a pair made during the Galloway artist Eric Booth Moodiecliffe's purple and blue period, ie during a time when he only had purple and blue paint.

At one time there was a coterie of artists working out of the Tam o Shanter in Dumfries. Prominent among these were Ronnie Fisher, a fisherman and painter transplanted from Newcastle, Frank Murphy a retired art teacher who did painfully intricate miniatures, Hugh MacIntyre, a proper professional painter widely acknowledged in this country and internationally and Eric Booth Moodiecliffe, an ex-mental nurse who had spent many years in Charters Towers in Australia and liked to paint historic landmarks. Ronnie and Eric were really only in it for beer and baccy money.

Ronnie was a proficient wildlife painter, who did a lot of stags and geese. Eric, I think it's fair to say, was a prolific but very bad painter. Opinions differed as to why this was, from the fact he was 'rushing it' or was too skint or mean to use a lot of paint, to the more widely held theory that he just had no talent for it whatsoever.

Eric was so world weary and likeable that he did shift some paintings, and whenever he sold one he would think he was onto a good thing and paint many other versions on the same theme. Therefore the selling of 'Cairnholy June 86' was followed by 'Cairnholy 2' all the way up to 'Cairnholy 9', all similar but as the series progressed with less and less paint. There was a kind of ghostly and other worldly aspect to these later paintings. I spoke to someone who owned 'Caerlaverock 8' who said there was now nothing at all on the canvas, and I often think this as the zenith of Eric's artistic career, kind of like Salvador Dali selling pictures with only a signature on them, only one step better.

Ronnie used to take the micky out of Eric's paintings, affectionately, because the two were good friends. Once, when a celebrity story was all over the newspapers concerning a drowning in a private swimming pool, Eric wondered aloud why the celebrity had a swimming pool since it was common knowledge he couldn't swim. 'Well' replied Ronnie in his thick Geordie accent, 'you've got paints!'

He was a rotten driver, too. We once went on a tour of the Machars in the course of which he nearly ploughed into a milk tanker. After we'd swerved into a lay-by he leaned across to me. 'Thank God I woke up in time' he whispered.

Eric was a beautiful poet and could recite long screeds of his own work, all from memory. As far as I know none of this was written down, and all has been lost, though he did go through a wee period of painting poems onto little canvases. Presumably they have all disappeared too. The only snatch that remains I wrote down, to try and capture in a poem the amazing story Eric once told me of nursing the American poet Robert Lowell after he had been committed in London.

Greenways, St John's Wood, 1970.
When Eric Booth Moodiecliffe enters,
Lowell is standing naked on the bed.
Moodiecliffe picks up the paper

discarded in panic by another nurse,
and begins to read.
After a minute, Lowell shouts
'Don't you know me?

I'm Robert Lowell, I'm famous!'
Folding the paper neatly on his lap
Moodiecliffe quietly says
'So? I'm better than you are.'

'Prove it' Lowell replies,
his face wax, wet with sweat.
Moodiecliffe then recites from memory
part of his epic poem set,

'Time is a Thief'.
'Time steals', he begins, 'that which anyone
would hold most dear...'
Soon, Lowell is shouting

'Moodiecliffe, you are one of the four
greatest poets since Shakespeare!'
By part six, however,
'as we must follow the wake of his insidious spoor',

Lowell is half dressed and
Moodiecliffe no better than Empson.
and as the clock strikes ten,
'borne along to that unknown

shore where night and darkness seal the door',
Lowell, clean shaven,
his hair combed and suitcase on the floor,
is asking, 'you finished with the paper?'

(The Healing Power of Poetry)

When Eric was drinking he'd mutter 'how would ye be?' in his quiet hybrid Australian accent. This would progress to 'who would you be?' then inevitably to 'why would you be?'

His was a rumpled and ultimately tragic life, looking back on it, but who am I to judge what counts as success?

Folk still talk about him, and I for my part am still searching for 'Midnight in Stavanger.'

Alba 3 An Òlaind 2

Màrtainn Mac an t-Saoir

San Albainn Nuaidh ud:
gheibh Eàirdsidh Gemmill am ball
còig slat air fhichead a-mach,
dannsaidh e seachad air Jansen e,
cuiridh e dà chois Khrol mu seach is mu làimh air a chorp,
putaidh e timcheall Phoortvliet e le snas na h-òrdaig,
ach 's ann nuair a thig Jongbloed – *gaolie* nan glùinean gòrach – thuige
a bhuaileas am fear beag againn lìon mòr ceannais. A-rithist 's a-rithist 's a-rithist!

Is ged a nì Johnny Repp an dèidh sin na nì e – is abair thusa eireachdas cràidh
chan eil e gu diofar, a chionn's gun do bheat sinn
Iran le sia agus sheall sinn samhla ùr dhan dùthaich roinnte sin
air deamocrasaidha tha fìor, fuasgailte, agus foghainteach.

Scotland 3 Holland 2

Martin MacIntyre

In that New Scotland:
Archie Gemmill gets the ball
twenty five yards out;
he dances it past Jansen,
sends both Krol's legs haplessly beyond his body,
nudges it round Poortvliet with perfect ballet-poise,
but it's when Jongbloed – the bound-knee'd keeper – makes his approach
that our wee fellow nets the great goal of responsibility. Again and again and again!

And though afterwards Johnny Repp does what he does – and so beautifully sore
it's not important, because we put six past Iran
and showed that riven country
a new model of democracy which is real, unrestricted and resolute.

Joha in Tamegroute

Wayne Price

The idiots and madmen of Tamegroute
are known to all the world of Islam
according to the Tuareg holy man
who keeps them calm.

In his indigo robe he tells them stories
of Joha the trickster hero, but tells me yes,
without question, if he could buy
drugs for them he would.

The middle-aged, bookish Californian
sharing the rooftop terrace
babbles in her sleep all night.
She tells me she dreams

of being operated on –
her parents the surgeons, herself
a child again – some minor procedure
she knows will kill her.

Here on the brittle rim of the Sahara
everything seems 'removed' to her.
Tired of being American, she scribbles
her thoughts each morning.

She would like to see the ancient,
animal-skin Qurans in the Zaouia,
but explains she has always been
frightened of simpletons.

Her schoolteacher daughter
from Portland lost patience – slipped
away to the long Atlantic breakers
and French boys at Essaouira. Lonely,

she quotes from everything
she reads: *The idea of a god*
who builds the universe to be
his own great gallows. Borges, she tells me.

My last day, shimmering noon,
a wandering patient plunged in front
of the Ouarzazate bus; it bounced him yards
but he sprang up miraculously unscratched.

Headstand, Naked

Wayne Price

The girl in the kitchen who stabbed
the margarine tub, then turned the knife
on me. Happy days! Midnight,
what a drive home that was: two pale

owls, huge, swift, ghostlike skimmed
the car. I swerved. Love, I love
the road that lengthens with each
moment we spend on it. A headstand

naked; all those quarrels and stories;
the shotgun broken and thrown in the pond;
the girl who liked sneezes; those owls;
the language that rescues love from us.

Increasing Caesura

Kirstie Allan

Much more likely you'll hurt me. Still what does it matter? If I've got to suffer, it may as well be at your hands, your pretty hands.
    Jean-Paul Sarte, *No Exit*

i.

i write entries in a diary after we meet. on monday 22nd july i wrote 'tectonic'
                                                                    and nothing else but
i can't remember what that was supposed to mean.

ii.

        we were strangers for far too long.   time for bravery.

iii.

sometimes i lose you for a bit. you're in the woods, i
guess.whole universes on top of you. i'm not going to
                            apologise any longer for looking
for you. i amn't going to be ashamed of being the one
who always texts first, or texts you   again. i
want you to know that i feel it. i hate games. i amn't
going to play with you. i won't wait four minutes to
text you back.   i'm still going to bring
a peanut butter kitkat chunky into your work
because it makes you smile. i'm working on my words.
'don't disappear', i say. you don't hear me. 'don't
disappear'. i'll tell you how important you are until
you become full of yourself. i'll save you   an esky
for when you need it. when i told how you my dad
orchestrated for my mum to be flown up from london
for their first date you said you loved it. you loved the
conspiracy to love. we go out dancing with friends
and find ourselves   dancing together. imagining

ourselves dancing over   paris. we have our own
asides. you are interesting and you make my life
interesting. the   first film we
fangirled over was *the wind rises.*   jiro says, 'the wind rises,
                                we must try to live'.

iv.

i don't want the easy road.

    fuck   the easy road.

    i want the   hard roads.   *all* of them.

    & all of their   silver   linings.

        because   let   me   tell   you,

            some   of   them   are   e x c e p t i o n a l.

Schrödinger's Playlist

Roddy Shippin

when you lean in close –
maze of hair, heat & smoke spirals,
rain bursting like static
& possibilities stretched each way

it's like that moment of tension
when the bassline to Walk On The Wild Side comes on
and there's still time for it to develop
into Can I Kick It

Belfast Bus

Jim Carruth

First bus of the day
half asleep mother
cleaner, cook, carer
wife, washerwoman
wage earner
a litany of roles
like rosary beads.
She complains
to her neighbour
curses fog and frost
the absence of the sun
her pale white skin;
words slip carelessly
as though on ice
what I really need
is one of those UVF lamps
and there it is said.
In the silence
you smell the burn
see the smoke.

Zweig

RA Davis

Telling me she'd read him, Sophia says
(in a Basel Swiss-German accent)

It's a lovely word: *zweig*. It means
you could say
a branch.

and this is what I see: a piece of green plastic foliage
we hang in our house at Christmas
which Mum calls a 'swag'

words bristle
and branch
and snag

Zweig

swag

twig

Tale of a Cosmic Crofter – No 4

Donald S Murray

His frigate-grey, fourth-hand Massey Ferguson
with its twenty horsepower, four cylinder engine
kept its wheels grounded for much of its existence,
surfing peat-bogs, testing out both wind and rain resistance
while heading out to machair, moor,
hauling trailers full of hay or seaweed from the shore,

Till the day the crofter bought it – and he found
its front-axle wheels could undertake a lift-off from the ground;
the mudguards above its rear wheels transmogrify to wings;
hydraulic system spinning; lynch pin
releasing it from hold and clutch of gravity.
A little choke and throttle and he could then break free

To regions where exhaust could funnel smoke
far away from neighbours as he journeyed through kaleidoscopes
and luminaries, escaping the bitter toil
experienced when he tilled and laboured on that fruitless soil.

The Apple Tree

Gerda Stevenson

After the phone call, they couldn't sleep. They lay in bed, husband and wife, eyes to the ceiling, fingers meshed. It was midwinter, and dawn would be late, so there was no hurry. They knew they'd be on the road in the morning, heading North, but couldn't face packing yet. Nothing to be done now, anyway. Iain's mother was gone. No warning. Her heart had stopped. She was still in bed, his brother had said, would stay there till the undertaker came. And that might be a while on Hogmanay.

Maria imagined her mother-in-law's cold limbs between the icy sheets. Wind from the Minch would be whistling up the croft, buffeting round the gable ends, rattling the windowpanes. The peat would still be glowing in the grate, the clock ticking on the mantelpiece. Her dog would know.

'Remember the picnic,' said Iain, reaching for the memory in the dark, 'when her daft dog protected those cooked chickens she'd bought? Ran like a bullet when that other mangy mutt appeared along the path. Never thought The Lump was capable of speed.'

Typical of Iain, thought Maria, to deflect from his pain with humour. He loved his mother, but could never speak of it.

'Yes,' she replied, 'that was a shining day, the picnic.'

Effie MacRae had been a widow most of her life. She was never extravagant. But she could surprise you, and splash out, as she did that day, when she slipped from Iain's car into the butcher's, and bought two whole chickens, roasted on a spit, dripping with warm, mouth-watering fat. And she always knew how to welcome you – scones and pancakes galore on arrival, crowdie from her own cow's milk, and jam, succulent with plump strawberries she'd tended and picked in her garden.

Effie's fingers weren't just green, Iain said – they were emerald, and her garden was the jewel of Braebac. That was where Maria first met her mother-in-law, on a still September afternoon, under the apple tree, the only one in the village. Effie was standing under its laden boughs, filling an old peat creel with the fruit, when Iain and Maria arrived. She gave one to Maria, who bit into its red skin, juice from the crisp, white flesh trickling down her chin. She'd never tasted such a delicious apple, sweet and subtly aromatic. She took three more from the creel, and to Effie's great delight, juggled them, right there, under the tree. And when Calum was born, Effie held her new grandson in her arms and sang *Craobh nan Ubhal* to him.

'It's about an apple tree,' Iain had told Maria. 'One of the oldest Gaelic songs – light years before Christ.'

Maria loved being married to a Gael, this big man, with a voice like peat. There was romance in the language, its lilt exotic compared to the flat tones of Surrey, where her own mother lived. She'd always felt rootless, an officer's only child, shipped around the colonies, and finally, when her parents separated, sent to boarding school in England. She hadn't known a feeling of community till she met Iain. Effie's island croft in the village of Braebac was an idyll in her mind; people dropped in and out of one another's houses with gifts – a bucket of fresh mackerel, or newly dug potatoes. And she never ceased to marvel at the box posted to their Edinburgh flat every month, a dozen Braebac eggs, each one swaddled in newspaper, perfectly intact.

'An idyll?' Iain would mock Maria's enthusiasm, 'a lethal concoction of church, gossip, and wall to wall TV soaps.' He never mentioned alcohol, the worm in the apple she tried to ignore, that she hadn't bargained for when they met. He'd been 'on the wagon' then.

He turned over in bed, away from her. 'I feel I'm disappearing,' he said, 'like one of your tricks.' His voice cracked through the dark, thinner than eggshell. 'I need a drink.'

'Can't we just lie quiet?' Maria asked, but he was already out of bed.

Two hours later, he stumbled back into the room, and flopped down beside her, snoring.

The forecast wasn't good next morning – snow from the West later in the day, so Maria got up early and packed the car, anxious to get on the road. Iain dragged himself out of bed, and charged himself with coffee before settling at the steering wheel. His eyelids drooped, and his face was as grey as the Firth of Forth.

'Are you sure you're up for driving, Iain?' Maria asked him.

'You mean, am I still pissed? Why don't you say what you're thinking?'

'I'm only offering – take it or leave it.'

'I've told you already, I'm fine,' he insisted. 'And anyway, it gives me something to do – I don't want to be just sitting for hours, with only Mum on my mind.'

Calum whimpered in the back.

'I've got something for you, darling!' Maria called to him over her shoulder, as she reached into her bag. 'Your favourite!' She slid a CD into the player on the dashboard.

'I can do without Postman bloody Pat right now, Maria,' groaned Iain. 'Specially in Gaelic. It's surreal.'

'I just thought... OK, we'll switch it off,' she sighed, pressing the stop button. Calum whimpered again. She reached into the back and stroked his small hand.

'He'll be asleep soon anyway,' said Iain. 'The car always sends him off.'

Maria looked out at the heavy clouds.

'Let's not try to fall out, love.'

'I'm not falling out. I told you, I'm fine.'

Calum began to snooze at last, and Maria gently extracted her hand from his.

'I fancy an apple,' she said, digging in her bag again. 'Do you want one?'

'No thanks.'

'Almost ten years since I met Effie,' said Maria, biting into the crisp, juicy flesh. 'D'you remember? Under the apple tree. That's the best painting you've ever done – the way you captured the moment, the autumn light. Perfect.'

'I'll never forget her face when you told her you were a magician,' Iain laughed dryly. 'Might as well have declared you were a Catholic. Don't think she ever got over it.'

'That's not true! She liked my juggling. And my handkerchief trick was her favourite – always asked me to do it!'

Maria watched Iain's hands on the steering wheel. Strong and earthy, yet elegant, with long fingers. An artist's hands, no doubt about it. She remembered him gutting a fish once, in Effie's kitchen sink, quick and firm, wielding the knife with breathtaking deftness. The same swift sweep she loved to watch when his paintbrush stroked a canvass – it made her dizzy, pierced the pit of her stomach.

'I failed her,' he said staring out through the windscreen. 'An artist, for God's sake, a graven image maker. And then I go and marry a magician. It's like I gave her the two fingers.'

'What do you mean!' Maria objected. 'She gave your apple tree painting pride of place in her house. She'd never have done that if she thought you were a failure.'

'A one-off. A lapse in faith on her part.'

Maria was losing patience. 'She loved you. You know she did.'

'Yes, but she'd have loved me more if I'd been a teacher, or a dentist, like Angus Morrison down the road – even a plumber, like James.'

'Don't be daft. She never loved James more than you.'

'I'm not so sure,' he replied. 'He's always been there for her – the 'good' son.'

'Maybe, but it was his choice – nobody asked him to build a house next door.'

'I'm just saying, he's been there for her, and I haven't.'

'Well, he never had to move away. When did anyone train to be an artist in Braebac?'

'I know, but she hated it. Art. Couldn't see the use in it. She has a point.'

'Had,' Maria corrected him. His negativity was getting to her.

'For fuck's sake,' he growled, 'no need to rub it in.'

'Sorry, love,' she said, resting her hand on his. 'I didn't mean – it's just when you get into this black denial of yourself, of what you do, what you are...'

'Just leave it – I'm driving!'

It came on her again, as it often did. A bleakness. They were so different – the attraction of opposites, she supposed. He was tall and dark, heavily built, with coiled hair that swept his shoulders like smoke. She was small and thin, her cropped blonde hair straight and spiked. A different landscape in their voices – in their minds too, she sometimes thought.

Snowflakes flecked the windscreen half way up the A9. An hour later the world was white.

'We won't make it to Braebac today,' said Iain, his focus on the road intense. 'Better stop at the first hotel that's open.'

Calum was awake, whimpering. Maria gave him some bread and juice. Then she rummaged in her bag for three tangerines, and juggled them to keep him entertained.

'Oranges in snow,' smiled Iain, 'I like that.'

He was hers again, he was with them. 'You should paint it,' said Maria.

'I might. Reminds me of home, when James and I were kids. Mum always gave us oranges at Hogmanay.'

They crawled along the road for another half hour, until a building loomed, just visible through the windscreen's sifting layers. The lettering on the sign was obliterated, but Iain drove in between the stately gateposts. The hotel seemed suspended, a ship afloat in snowfall. Festive lights looped around the eaves, and the windows throbbed with warmth. A huge snowman stood in the car park, sporting a black top hat, pipe in mouth, and an arm that curved to his hip like the handle of a jaunty teapot.

'D'you think he's the proprietor?' Iain joked, lifting Calum up to the mute face.

'Mummy's hat!' said the little boy.

'Yes, it's just like mine,' laughed Maria, 'Maybe there's a rabbit inside!' and she raised the brim for Calum to have a peek.

'All gone,' he piped, 'all gone!'

'Let's hope there's room at the inn,' said Iain, as they stamped snow from their shoes on the entrance hall mat.

A friendly young woman in a tartan skirt led them upstairs. They threaded their way along a tartan-carpeted corridor, past a stuffed fox in a glass case, to a vacant family room. It was small, but comfortable, and they were soon installed. Maria played with Calum on the bed, while Iain filled the kettle and laid out cups.

'Did you ring the theatre?' he asked.

'Yes. I called first thing. They'll get the understudy in.'

Miraculous Maria playing the Fairy Godmother was about as remote as Mars right now. The building was quiet, no sound from other rooms, the air outside hushed, as if a blanket had descended for miles around. 'It doesn't seem real,' she thought.

'It's like we're in some strange time zone,' said Iain, reading her mind.

He crossed to the window and stared out at the shrouded dusk. 'No-one in the world but us.'

They ordered supper to be brought to their room.

'Shouldn't we ring James, tell him we won't be there tonight?' suggested Maria.

'You do it. I don't want to speak to him right now. And I couldn't face Ishbel if she picks up the phone.'

Maria felt Iain was a bit hard on his sister-in-law. It wasn't Ishbel's fault that she hadn't had much of an education. 'Rubbish,' he'd say. 'She was born like that. I pity anyone who tries to open a door in *her* closed mind. You'd need a crowbar.'

Ishbel's voice crooned down the line from Braebac: 'Oh, dear, that's a shame. You'll miss seeing Effie, then. The undertakers are coming this evening.'

'Couldn't they wait till tomorrow?' asked Maria.

'I don't think so, dear. We can't have the remains lying in the house for another night.'

The remains? Maria pictured a bin-bag of leftover spare ribs picked at by crows on the roadside.

'Iain really wants to see his mother one last time,' she insisted, 'and so do I.'

'Well, that may be,' Ishbel nipped, 'But it's not the way we do things here.'

'Can I have a word with James?' Maria asked, rolling her eyes in Iain's direction.

'Told you,' he mouthed from the bed, where Calum slept in his arms.

'Well, alright – if you want,' Ishbel relented, 'but I don't think he'll say any different.'

'No problem,' James slurred. 'I'll sort it out.'

Maria tidied Calum's clothes, and began to get ready for bed.

'I'm going to the bar for a dram,' said Iain.

Her heart sank. She didn't want their cocoon to be breached, this little bit of consolation from the weather god. 'You could ask room service to bring one up for you. I love it in here, just the three of us.'

But he was already on his way out.

'It's Hogmanay, for Christ's sake! I think a dram and some company might be in order.'

Maria watched the door close behind him. She reached for the remote, and switched on the TV. Celebrity revellers roared at a joke she'd just missed. She snapped it off. The bleakness had descended again. Suddenly she longed for her mother's voice, reserved, caring, reliable. Then she realised she hadn't told her that Effie had died. In their hurry to leave Edinburgh before the snow came, she'd forgotten to call her. She picked up the phone and dialled Surrey, but it rang out, and the voicemail clicked on:

'Please speak after the bleep.'

It didn't seem right to leave news of death on an answerphone. Maria found herself saying in a shockingly perky voice:

'Happy New Year for tomorrow, Mum – or *Bliadhna Mhath Ur*, as they say up here!'

The sky was clear in the morning, and the roads were black again. The snow ploughs had done their work. Calum waved to the snowman as they drove off.

'Happy Year!' he sang out.

'I wish you'd speak Gaelic to him,' said Maria. 'I love to hear it on the phone when you talk to your...'

'To my Mum, yes, I know. Gaelic's going the same road as her. If it's not dead, it's dying.'

'I don't see why. I mean, you could start speaking it with James. You both spoke Gaelic to Effie.'

'Yes, but never at school.'

'What – not even in the playground?'

'No. So why would we bother now?'

'For Calum. I'd like him to know it.'

'I'm telling you, it's had its day.'

'Oh, right,' said Maria, resorting to sarcasm, 'so you're saying it's inevitable?'

'As inevitable as the melting snow,' sighed Iain, weary of the subject.

'Or your love affair with alcohol.'

There was a pause as they both took in what she'd just said. Then Iain rammed his foot down on the accelerator.

'My mother may be dead, but by God, Maria, she's alive in you!'

The ferry wasn't running on New Year's Day, so Iain had called a friend who'd agreed to take them across on a small one-man ferry he operated during the summer months. They reached Braebac by mid afternoon. Once he'd switched off the ignition, Iain stayed in the driver's seat for a moment, looking at the house. Peat smoke rose from the chimney, as it always did, whatever the season. Its thick, sweet scent hung on the damp air and seeped into the car as Maria opened the passenger door. A strange noise came with it, a low moan, barely audible. She glanced at Calum, but he was asleep in the back. Then she realised. It was Iain. He was crying, but she hadn't recognised the signs, because she'd never seen him do it before. He held out his hand and she took it in hers.

'I just ca... can't' he stammered, 'just can't... oh, God...'

Every chair in the sitting room was taken. Ishbel was bustling about, serving scones and pancakes to neighbours. James was dispensing drams. Broc, otherwise known as The Lump, moped at the hearth. The greetings were sombre and brief.

'Go on up,' James said to Iain. 'She's still in her room. Leave Calum down here with us.'

Together they climbed the stairs. Iain paused on the landing by the mahogany tallboy, and brushed a finger across the huge, dusty bible laid out on top – the only book in the house.

Maria leaned into his shoulder. 'Will we go in, love?'

'Aye,' he nodded.

The window was ajar, and the closed curtains billowed gently. Low winter light filtered through their thin folds, rippling over Effie's face. The bed appeared to be almost rocking, like a submerged boat just below the sea's translucent surface. A trick of light washed the years from the old woman's high, wide brow, erased the lines beneath her eyes, and filled out her sunken cheeks. She looked like a sleeping, grey-haired girl, hands crossed above her breast.

'A mhathair, mo ghraidh,' murmured Iain, as he knelt beside the bed, laying a hand on hers.

Maria had enough Gaelic to know he'd found the words at last to tell his mother he loved her.

The clock on the sitting room mantelpiece chimed seven, and a sleek black car purred down the track. The undertakers had arrived. Iain and James helped them carry the coffin downstairs and out into the dark. The heart had gone from the house, it seemed.

Maria began to get Calum ready for bed.

'I'll take Broc for a walk,' Iain said to her. 'Poor old Lump – he looks lost.'

By half past eight Maria was snuggled under the duvet, reading a story to Calum. Iain came upstairs and sat on the bed with them.

'It's cold out,' he said, stroking Calum's forehead. 'Lots of stars.'

The child smiled and slipped into sleep.

Maria whispered, not to wake him. 'It's weird, isn't it, being in the house without her.'

'I know,' Iain nodded. 'You can feel the emptiness pressing through the walls.'

'Iain!' Ishbel's voice split the quiet air. 'Iain? That's the elders coming now! Time you were down!'

He got up from the bed. 'God, that woman. The sensitivity of a clootie dumpling.'

'Why have the elders come?' Maria asked.

'What do you think? To pray for our souls. That's what they do here – gather at the house, every night till the day of the funeral. Small chance any of us'll make it through the pearly gates, though – even Mum, no matter how hard she tried. And, by God, she tried.'

'Should I come down with you?' asked Maria.

'It'll be all men. You might feel a bit like a fish out of water.'

'What about Ishbel?'

'She'll be in the kitchen, buttering pancakes and cream crackers for them all.'

'I might make an appearance in my cloak of invisibility,' she smiled.

'Wouldn't work,' he twinkled in that dark way of his she loved. 'The Mullahs of Braebac have x-ray eyes.'

'What about supper?'

'Don't worry. Kate next door's just been round with soup and sandwiches, and buckets of scones.'

Then he turned at the door and grinned, 'We'll dine when the hoodie crows have gone!'

Maria switched off the light, and lay in the dark next to Calum. Gaelic psalms floated up from the sitting room below – the human voice reaching out, enfolding. Strange music, this, she thought – unaccompanied, austere, yet elaborate with its own adornment, notes twisting around themselves like golden knots. She'd never been particularly religious. Her parents had taken her to church once in a while, during holidays from boarding school – Church of England, a gentle affair, the three of them standing there, singing – that's all she could remember about it. But her mother stopped going when the marriage broke down. Nevertheless, Maria always felt vaguely attracted to the idea of religion, the opportunity of ritual, faith in the unknown. 'It's the magician in you,' Iain would tease her. 'All that hocus pocus.' She knew that Iain and Effie hadn't seen eye to eye on such matters, though she'd never really understood why. After all, she thought, there was a fierce warmth here, a deep comfort in the way these people gathered around their bereaved, and nursed them through the shadow of loss; something atavistic, necessary, solid as rock. She felt proud that this was part of her son's inheritance.

She missed pottering about the croft with Effie, and didn't feel welcomed by her in-laws, who seemed to have moved in for the time being. Effie's cow, Nancy, was old now, and dry, so there was no milking to be done, but Calum enjoyed feeding the hens, collecting eggs in a basket. Maria took him out to the garden one morning.

'No flowers – all gone!' he said, practising his favourite phrase.

'They're just asleep,' she explained, leading him to Effie's apple tree. They stood under its bare winter branches, and Calum stroked the bark.

'Apple tree,' said Maria. '*Craobh nan ubhal*. Can you say that?'

'Coo nan ool,' he cooed, enjoying the sound.

Back in the sitting room, she held him up to Iain's painting, and pointed to the tree.

'Coo nan ool,' he said again and again, 'coo nan ool!'

'You see,' Maria smiled at Iain, 'your son's learning Gaelic!'

'Thought he was talking about Nancy the Coo,' said Iain, not looking up from his book.

The elders came round for four nights. As soon as they'd gone, James switched on the TV and cracked open the whisky. The brothers would sit in silence, glued to the screen, watching the snooker, eating supper and downing drams, while their wives dined in the kitchen. Maria wondered about the funeral arrangements, what to do with Calum.

'Kate's daughter next door will have him,' said Ishbel, chewing on a ham sandwich.

'Can we help in any way?' offered Maria. 'Organising things...'

'Don't worry, it's all in hand.'

'Well, we'll obviously contribute to the cost.'

Ishbel gave no response.

'Do you think I could perhaps say a few words at the service?' Maria asked. 'Something about Effie, and her garden – the apple tree?'

Ishbel almost choked on her sandwich. 'Goodness, no!' she coughed, and took a slug of tea to clear her throat. 'The ministers will be dealing with all of that!'

Mist came in from the North on the day of the funeral. Stray snow wreathes lay tucked in folds by the hillside path that led to the church. Maria stood with Iain, three rows from the front. 'I'm damned if I'll stand in the firing line,' he'd hissed at Ishbel, when she'd tried to usher him into the front, next to her and James.

Maria had never been to this church before. Its Spartan appearance surprised her. The damp, whitewashed walls were bare, the floor covered in cracked linoleum. The congregation was a sea of black, every pew filled. There was no organ, no music to ease the atmosphere.

'Where's the coffin?' Maria asked Iain.

'Out in the hallway, by the front door.'

'Yes, but...they're bringing Effie in, aren't they?'

Iain gave a wry laugh. 'This isn't about her.'

'What do you mean? Of course it is!' Maria protested.

'I think you'll find it isn't. Look – here they come, the hoodie crows.'

Three ministers took their places by the pulpit, perched like ravens.

'We're in for a treat,' Iain muttered, 'a stiff triple measure. We'll all be on the floor.'

His cheek muscles twitched the way they always did when he was tense. Maria slipped her hand into his as the first of the ministers stepped up. She listened, but his words didn't make sense. They were so far from what she'd expected that she couldn't immediately decode their meaning. To her utter astonishment, she realised that this gaunt stranger was haranguing her, accusing her, and everyone gathered there, of not attending church as often as they should. She suppressed an instinct to heckle, to challenge his presumption – how did *he* know when she last went to church? And if he wasn't referring to her, then why wash the parish's dirty linen in public, today, of all days? Didn't this man know that people had travelled a long way to celebrate Effie's life? He was talking of fires being kindled by Jehovah's breath, like a stream of brimstone, he said, condemning them all to hell for their sins, even for being born, it seemed. Each head was bowed in submission, a pool of unbearable shame. Hail beat on the high, arched windows, and the minister raised his voice, relishing the contest. A shiver rippled through the congregation, as if it had blurred into one creature. Then the hail subsided, and sunlight pierced the gloom – a single beam resting on the nape of Ishbel's neck. Maria wanted to reach out and kiss it, tell her sister-in-law to hold her head high. When would these holy men begin to talk about Effie, speak her name? When would words of comfort be offered, thanks given for her life, the woman they'd all known and loved? The second minister was speaking now, voice like a bull. He rocked rhythmically from side to side, and the floorboards creaked. Maria heard mention of a tree, an apple tree, in a beautiful garden – Effie's garden, she thought, tears of relief welling in her eyes. Effie's apple tree, *Craobh nan Ubhal*. But, no, that wasn't it – he was talking of Eden. The sin of Eve – the apple she plucked from the tree to poison the world with knowledge. Maria looked at Iain. His face was so white his features seemed to have melted.

The day felt like a shipwreck. Somehow Iain managed to play his part, shouldered the coffin with the pallbearers up to the cemetery, and took his place at the graveside. Maria straggled behind the procession of men, the only woman among them, but she didn't care what they thought. She watched Iain as he held one of the cords and lowered his mother into the earth.

The last of the mourners had left Effie's house. Maria and Ishbel were in the sitting room, clearing up, Iain and James glued to their armchairs, opening another bottle of whisky. The atmosphere was like a loaded gun. Ishbel fired the first shot.

'I don't know what you were thinking, Maria, going to the graveside – it just isn't done. Didn't you tell her, Iain?'

'He told me, Ishbel,' said Maria , quietly intervening.

'Course I *told* her!' Iain flung the word over his shoulder. 'But she's a grown up. Her choice.'

'It's nothing to do with choice,' Ishbel insisted.

James leaned across the hearth to fill up his brother's glass.

'I'm afraid,' he mumbled, with a weak, conspiratorial smile, 'it's a case of 'when in Rome'...'

'Didn't know you'd turned Catholic, James!' Ishbel chastised her husband. 'It's about respect. For how we do things here.'

'Iain needed me, Ishbel,' Maria explained. 'The service wasn't exactly comforting. It was...I mean, no mention of Effie, her life...it could have been *anyone's* funeral!'

'It's not for the deceased,' replied Ishbel, her anger rattling the teacups as she cleared them onto a tray.

'Or the living,' Iain laughed to himself. 'No siree!'

'A funeral's a warning, a warning to us all,' Ishbel continued, cleaving to her dignity.

Maria knew she should let it alone, but somehow she couldn't. 'Well, it wasn't easy to get through.'

'It's not *meant* to be easy!' Ishbel insisted.

'You're right there!' thundered Iain, rising from his chair. 'It's what it's meant to be – a crucifixion of your feelings, a slaughter of your bloody soul. Spiritual fascism, that's what it is!'

James hauled Iain back into his seat. 'Wheesht, Iain! You'll be getting yourself snookered, talking like that – snookered, just!'

'Your brother's a disgrace, James,' said Ishbel, piling sherry glasses on top of the wobbling teacups.

'It's only the drink talking, ' James reassured her, 'that's all. Only the drink.'

'Will you listen to the pot calling the kettle!' she hit back.

'Why don't you two bugger off home to your own house and leave us in peace?' growled Iain.

Maria put her hand on his shoulder: 'Iain! Please, love...'

'Come on now, let's all calm down,' said James. 'A bit of relaxation... how about one of your tricks, Maria? That one you do with the hanky, eh?'

'For goodness sake!' spluttered Ishbel, disgusted.

James reached into his pocket. 'I've got one here somewhere.' He swayed on his feet as he dug deep, and pulled out a crumpled grey rag. 'There you go!' he said, triumphantly, presenting it to Maria. 'Can you make it disappear?'

Maria took the thing, but couldn't think what to say.

'Smashing!' laughed James, rubbing his palms in what seemed to be genuine anticipation. 'Let's watch the magic, then! Go on, Maria! Go on!'

'Well... I... I... alright,' she stammered, 'if you... if you're sure you really... Abradadabra...,' and gave the cloth a feeble flourish. James exploded with drunken laughter:

'Will you look at that! Did you see that? It's gone! My flipping hanky's gone!'

'What are you thinking, James!' gasped Ishbel, slamming down the tray, sherry glasses and teacups rolling onto the table, 'and your mother just buried! Give that filthy article back to him, Maria, wherever you've put the horrible thing!'

Iain had sunk forward in his chair, his head in his hands.

'This is unbelievable!' he moaned, rocking back and forward.

'Would... would anyone like a cup of tea?' ventured Maria.

'Never mind tea,' said Ishbel, thumping the crockery back onto the tray. 'There's all these sherry glasses and plates to tidy up first.'

Iain leapt to his feet again and lunged at the table.

'I'll tidy up your damned sherry glasses for you!' he roared, sweeping the lot to the floor.

They stood for a moment in silence. Broken glass and china twinkled among the cold tea puddles soaking into the carpet.

'That man of yours is totally out of control, Maria,' said Ishbel, with a terrifying calm that defied response. 'I'll clear this mess. You'd better go and pick up your child from next door. I expect they'll have had enough of him by now.'

Later that afternoon, Maria was peeling potatoes at the kitchen sink, Calum babbling at her feet. She heard the front door slam, so hard the walls shook. She went through to the sitting room. Only a few minutes ago, Iain had been stretched out on the sofa, snoozing, but he was gone. James was slumped in Effie's armchair, staring at the peat flames, and Ishbel was standing in the middle of the room, strangely still, a piece of paper in her hand.

'Is everything alright?' asked Maria.

Without a word, Ishbel handed her the paper. It was Effie's will. The simple statement made it clear that everything had been left to James.

'Would you mind watching Calum for me?' Maria asked, handing the piece of paper back to Ishbel. 'I have to see if Iain's alright.'

'Aye,' mumbled James, through a whisky haze. 'No problem.'

Iain stood alone on the brae, a silhouette in the dusk. Maria caught up with him, and they continued along the track in silence for a while. At last she spoke:

'I read it. The will. Did you know?'

He walked on a few paces before he replied.

'No.'

She thought she detected a tremor in the single word, but had never seen him more dignified.

'No,' he said again, 'I didn't.'

They were heading along the top road now, Effie's house below them, the croft sweeping to the shore like a brown winter blanket.

'Did I ever tell you,' said Iain, 'you can't say 'to own' in Gaelic? We don't have that verb. The concept doesn't exist.'

'So what do you do then? Share, lend?'

'Not with Ishbel and James, you don't. But way back, a hundred years ago, yes – folk took turns – a rolling system, where you each had a shot at the good land.'

Maria looked down at Effie's house again, its whitewashed walls a dim eye in the fading light. 'It's the garden that breaks my heart,' she said. 'The apple tree. Not being able to come here and pick apples with Calum. Why on earth…? Was it what you said – the graven images, and marrying me?'

'It didn't help, but no, it wasn't that.'

'Well, what then?'

'She was right,' said Iain, looking towards the headland as they walked on. 'From her point of view, she was right. I'm not a believer. Never could be. And I told her so. It was a good few years back – before I met you. I told her because I couldn't pretend any more. I didn't sign up, so she wrote me out.'

Maria had been married to this man for almost a decade. It was only now that she was beginning to understand him.

'But everything?' she persisted. 'Everything? It's so extreme.'

He gave a bleak little laugh. 'Extreme is the word for normal here.'

They packed their things next morning.

'I'll drive,' Maria told him. 'You can sleep off your hangover.'

He didn't object, merely pointed out that although he'd come to bed late, he hadn't been drinking, actually. 'There was a full moon, white as a pandrop, and I went for a walk,' he said. 'Wanted to have a look at Braebac in a new light. Nearly woke you up to get you to come with me.'

'And what did Braebac look like?' she asked.

'Not home anymore.'

He was keen to be on the road. He'd strapped Calum into the back, and planted himself in the passenger seat with his newspaper, long before Maria was ready. Inside the house, she gathered the toys from the sitting room floor. James and Ishbel sat at the kitchen table, finishing breakfast in silence. Maria picked up her bags, and took them out to the car.

'That you?' Iain asked. 'Are we off, then?'

'Yes, that's me.' She settled herself into the driver's seat, and switched on the ignition, but didn't drive off.

'What are we waiting for?' Iain yawned. 'Come on. Let's get going.'

Maria opened the door, and got out of the car, the engine still running.

'There's something I need – won't be a minute,' she called, and ran back into the house.

Ishbel was on her knees in the sitting room, raking ashes at the hearth.

'Have you forgotten something?' she asked – the first time she'd spoken to her sister-in-law since she'd handed her the will the day before.

Maria took off her shoes. 'Yes. I have. The apple tree.'

She stood on the sofa, and lifted Iain's painting from its hook on the wall.

'Don't James and I own that?' said Ishbel, a statement behind the question.

'I don't think so,' replied Maria. 'And anyway, it's our turn now.'

'Hope you won't take after your mother,' Iain winked at Calum, as they drove up the hill out of Braebac. 'Cinneach, that's what she is!'

'Coo nan ool!' Calum cooed, pointing at the painting, perched on the back seat next to him.

'Aye, that's right,' Iain nodded, 'Craobh nan Ubhal. And your mother's a cinneach! Mind that word, Calum – cinneach!'

'That wouldn't be you speaking Gaelic to your son?' smiled Maria.

'Keenyach! Keenyach!' Calum crooned.

'That's it!' laughed Iain. 'A heathen! She's obviously never heard of the eighth commandment – nothing but a thieving heathen!'

Statutory Right

Danni Glover

You are sixteen going on seventeen
Fellows will fall in line
Eager young lads and rogues and cads
Will offer you food and wine.

Forgive me if I'm not enthusiastic
That the girl you're with still looks like her school photo
That she giggles as you pour her vodka lemonade
That you told her that you loved her the second time you met.
I could see her spilling splinters of self esteem.

You know, she loaned me a novel –
I found it kind of puerile –
About a young woman who is made to feel special
By a boy who has no acne and whose favourite book is *The Catcher in the Rye*.
I guess I'd see it.
If I were younger I'd feel lucky
To be kissed by a man who had kissed women.
Then I'd know I was a woman.
I'd be fierce and complicated and uncompromising,
That's the problem with women. All the trying.

Tell me,
Why'd you go to bed with a teenage girl?
Is it because they open shyly like a wound
With no hard scar tissue?
Are they more fun to stick it into?
Do they not argue?
Do they like Tarantino films as much as you do?
When you upset them, do they say 'I' more than they say 'You'?
Are they easier to lie to?
Do they breathe in the things they should see through?
Do they taste new?
When you fuck them, do they thank you?

Do they bruise,
And are they excited because you brought booze?
Do they think less?
Do they talk less?
When you come over, is their bedroom a mess?
Does it feel like there's less to invest?
Are they a good placebo for loneliness?
Do they have to get home early to study for a test?
Do they have nice breasts?
Don't they get stressed?
Are there kisses at the end of all of their texts?
Is their confidence in shreds
Because of something that *bitch* said?
Does that make it easy to take them to bed?
Do they give head?
Do they not demand head?
Do they make you forget that one day you'll be dead?
Are they good for your street cred?
Have you told your friends?
Will you wed them?
Do they expect you to wed them?
Are they enlightened about feminism?
Have they been corrupted by feminism?

Tell me,
What drugs are they into these days?
What music?
What do they find ironic?
Tell me,
Why'd you go to bed with a teenage girl?

Let me tell you something about agency.
Agency is like pubic hair:
When you're that age there isn't as much there
And you haven't decided what to do with it yet.
So what?
Age is just a number
Just like prison's just a room
Just like hell is just a storage heater underneath your tomb.

I get the feeling this is going to go horribly wrong
A selfish kind of clinging to my own childhood and hers.
I remember my own idiocy
And the soft, new growths of my own body
And insecurity.
I remember the things that men would say to me.

Tell me.
Why'd you go to bed with a teenage girl?

The Zaps

Dorothy Lawrenson

5am is a bad joke

       6 an accusation

you've got to think on your feet

and just because you're paranoid the barman says
why the long face?

you hope you're not getting ill again
I hope you're not getting ill again

    did you hear about
the man

/

if you miss a pill you start to feel the zaps
paddy dies and goes to heaven and
when he reaches the pearly gates St Peter says
I told you I was ill

/ what's black and white and eats like a horse?

little \ electric \ shocks to the head

             7am is waiting for a punchline

what's the difference between Bing Crosby and
the pope dies and goes to heaven and when he gets to the pearly gates
and what's the difference? It's not like you to throw up
and what's the difference?
three Methodists walk into a bar
a horse walks into a bar
an Englishman, an Irishman and a Scotsman
either sleep too much or not at all

you've got to think on your feet

did you hear about the magic tractor?

\ and not eating

I heard you last night
did you hear about the man?
I never heard about the man
Did you hear about the woman?

/ a zebra /

Use your imagination
Use your imagination
Use your imagination

the barman says is this some kind of a joke?

The Ingenious Gentleman of La Mancha Hung Over the North Sea

William Bonar

Metal throbs at layered,
interfering frequencies
through bones and skull.

Vomit is convulsed
into brown paper bags.

Feavered sweat pools
inside survival suits.

Bowels shift, are clenched,
eyes ache, restless, unsalved.

Still this windmill thuds
towards fiery iron giants
thigh deep in greasy seas.

Fix horizon! Lower lance!

A Thrawn Tryst

Pippa Little

In white rain a crow keeps to its own shadow
sleeking low over us, silent
but for the wet beat of its cloven wings.
Moor and rough pasture, willow and alder,
bog-myrtle, rosemary, buzzard and adder,
I, Flodden, was the old floor, commonplace, until
this hour of last, smirring light
when your stocking-feet ploutered me to glaur,
scuddied in bloody glit my soft moss skin
till I'm broken as you are broken, slit through
by bill and pike to sprauchle in flesh and loam
and gone beyond all knowing -
I grasp you, pull you down,
we twist like thrawn lovers, dogs
that bare their jaws at another's throat.
James Scrimgeour, Richard Clemenger,
we cannot be harmed or pitied now:
everything that hurts
roots, ingrows,
a sob fisted deep in the thrapple.

James Scrimgeour of Glassary, Argyllshire and Richard Clemenger, Englishman, both died at Flodden. The battleground was
so slippery that many kicked off their shoes in order to get a better grip as they fought hand-to-hand.

Ghazal

Rizwan Akhtar

(after Faiz Ahmad Faiz*)

However the lamp's wick is chirping in the swelling night
One man and one metaphor can also make a tale out of night.

I don't want the day's dazzling candour, I don't want clarity
the darkness and silence makes brighter my night.

Why ask for the sun? Your cheek is burning in my lap
a scribe, a blacksmith, a digger can make something of night.

Look at the scales tilting in favour of the big tribes
One pull, one vibration from the distant hand of night

the moon hanging over the Fort's chipped merlons
dies down there in my palms you sleep and cry in night

you're an idea, my love, what else is but plight
Just mentioning you would make verse envious of night.

Angels can wait to have wings clean for the next flight
this pen, makes me earth-bound for the night

I've no pleas to make, as Faiz says to himself
isn't it enough to speak about the night?

* Faiz Ahmad Faiz (1911 – 1984), winner of the Lenin Peace Prize, was a well-known Urdu language poet in Pakistan.

The Delay

Cynthia Rogerson

The announcement said there would be a further delay. Joanna asked her husband:

'Fancy a coffee and one of those funny almond cakes?'

'Nah. Out of Euros, no point in getting more now.' George was a big man, with thin grey hair, and his scalp shone through.

It didn't really matter about the coffee or the cake. She always packed a little snack for the journey home. Now was not quite the right time. Pacing oneself, that was the key to life. She began to read a magazine.

No one in the airport took notice of them. Mostly, no one seemed to notice anyone. There was a family who all wore crocs of different colours on their sunburned feet. An old German woman in a wheelchair, and her daughter yawning behind her. A couple from Holland, the girl straddling the boy's lap, both looking innocent as children in pyjamas, bathed and ready for bed.

There were dozens of similar groups, all in their own orbits. Not to mention the stag and hen parties, hung-over and beyond speech, the imminent brides and grooms numbly anticipating their nuptials. Oh, and there was a man with no shoes. He was wandering from group to group, talking in Russian to no one in particular. The words had the tone of a rant, but his gestures were limp and mild. You could tell he'd been a beautiful boy. There was something appealing even in his self-neglect. A modesty. He carried no bag, not even a backpack, and smelled of unwashed groin.

Joanna saw some of this, quickly, hardly needing to glance up. Like some richly textured drowsy music in the background, interesting enough to tune into, but easy to tune out. The Russian felt threatening, but not overtly so. She finished an article about Agas, and began another about healthy alternatives to hormone replacement therapy. The delay was annoying. She'd already imagined their arrival home by tea time, the kettle whistling, the tail-wagging dogs. She'd rehearsed her anecdote about George and the jellyfish. She could feel it like a delicious bubble inside herself; it took up physical space, aching to be told. She'd delete the boring lead up and cut straight to his bare ass with the red welts, and the group of old women screaming and giggling. He'd blamed her, of course. She'd have to wait for the right audience. Someone he liked too much to show his angry self to. She'd get him to laugh about it too, finally.

'What do you think will happen?' she asked him.

'Eh?'

'What about all the backed up flights? Is the sky full of planes waiting to land?'

'How the hell should I know?'

'Now George, no need to get snappy.'

'I'm going to the loo.'

'I will too.'

'No, you stay. We'll lose our seats otherwise.'

It was true. There were more people than seats.

She watched him walk away, and with the sight of his sunburned neck, her irritation melted. He was just tired. She put her magazine down and looked at their bags, hats, sunglasses, tidily piled up to take up as little space as possible. Ah, marriage! After thirty years, it still surprised her sometimes. She'd grown up imagining it so differently. And here they were, and this was her marriage. She looked at her watch. She looked at the advertisements on the wall for soft drinks and Sea World, all in English. And towards the glass doors, through the fog at rows of buses. And at the small kiosk selling coffee and almond cakes and ice creams, and the tobacconist selling sweets and newspapers and cigarettes. It felt like she'd been in the airport a week. More familiar than their little hotel room by the beach. More familiar, in fact, than her own kitchen.

He returned. The way that man could make every facial muscle droop! She told her heart not to sink, but it did anyway. Maybe it was simply that they'd been alone for an entire week. Maybe they needed... diluting. He sat down heavily and she said:

'I'm going to the loo now.'

'Good luck,' he said dully.

She followed the signs to the toilet. There was a long queue. She settled into a trance-like state, trying to find a place to put her gaze that avoided other women's eyes. She saw herself in the mirror and suddenly remembered being in this same place a week ago, thinking – *I look so old*. She wore her holiday dress, one she never wore at home. She loved it, and even now found herself admiring the scoop neck exposing her tanned skin, the warm pattern of yellow roses on red cotton.

When it was her turn, the toilet was blocked and filthy. She squatted over the seat. No toilet paper, so she wiped herself with a bit of scrap paper. The taps weren't working; she used a wet wipe. She returned to George, smiling, proud of her empty bladder and clean hands.

'I think the sun is starting to break through. Anyway, the fog is quite nice, don't you think? A change from all that blinding heat.'

'Jesus. Can you stop being so bloody cheerful for just two minutes?'

She opened her mouth as if to speak, then closed it. Sat down heavily, sighed and let the old silence gather.

'Toilet working ok?'

'Uhuh,' she replied flatly.

'Oh now Jo, don't start sulking. Why can't you just admit some things are terrible?'

She felt her throat swell. She corralled her voice, commanded it not to wobble.

'Because it doesn't help. Moaning does not help.'

'Where are you going now?'

She heard him but kept walking. Imagined finding a bus to town, learning Greek, getting a job as a waitress, living in a tiny whitewashed room. For a second, she let this vision wash through her. The single toothbrush, the whole expanse of bed. She'd sit in the shade of cafes and read Thomas Hardy, and eat nothing but fish and salads and fruit. She would sip espressos in the morning, and red wine as the sun set. People would think she was mysterious and interesting. Damn him! Damn damn damn this fog, and damn the sun before it.

They were just tired.

They needed to be home now. And of course, they *would* be home soon, before they knew it, and this airport would be full of other tourists. Thinking this, helped somehow. This time tomorrow – same place, different people. The world didn't just have herself and her husband in it. All those other people and their worlds, every bit as real. She felt the heaviness slide away again.

She strolled outside for air, but the fog was oppressive and smelly, like foreign cigarettes. Breathing took effort. She wandered slowly, feeling invisible. She watched women lift their children behind a palm tree, cradle them so their bare bottoms hung down. Three palms away, older kids kicked empty beer tins or chased each other. She noticed smokers clumped together under the awnings, using empty crates for seats. A bottle was being passed round and their smoke hung like a curtain, separating them from more wholesome tourists.

She wandered back inside, noticed routines forming here too. Families sprawled, suitcases spilling out beach clothes. An air of home-like squalor. People were talking loudly, laughing, snoring or tapping into their phones. She was a nurse; she imagined taking the blood pressure of this room. Low, almost unhealthily low.

Then the crackle that meant an announcement was imminent, and everyone quietened.

'Attention please. Atencióne! Due to the weather, all flights are cancelled.' Crackle. 'No flights tonight from this aeroporto. British Airways passengers are asked to go to the exit doors for the hotel bus.' Crackle. 'British Airways passengers only.'

Silence. Crackle again. Then as if someone had responded, the voice continued.

'Yes, this is very.' Crackle. 'Unfortunate.'

Joanna glanced across the terminal and noticed George opening his eyes. He looked startled, exposed. It was like catching a glimpse of herself unexpectedly, and she rushed back to him.

'Great!' he burst out the instant he saw her. 'Marvellous.'

'I know, I know,' she cooed, moving a carrier bag to sit next to him. It was strangely comforting now, to hear him grumble. He wound down and they sat in silence, completely still, while around them groups conferred, parted, re-grouped, spread out. This was just a temporary blip. Their lives were on *pause*, exactly like a dvd. Soon, they would be on *play* again. But wasn't it a fact: one day their lives would simply *stop*? She turned to George, touched his arm. Noted he needed a shave.

About sixty passengers filed out of the terminal into a coach, guided by cool young women holding clip boards.

'There go the BA folk, lucky bastards. That's the class system for you.'

'Yes. Look at them,' she said, rummaging in her bag for another magazine.

'Go on, abandon us, you traitors!'

'Off to your nice hotel rooms.' It was oddly fun, now and then, to be sarcastic like him. And oddly easy.

'Your soft beds and clean toilets.'

'I hope you get pneumonia from the air conditioning!'

'I'll get us some food,' he said suddenly. 'Sandwiches, maybe a beer. I'll use my card.'

She thought of the sandwiches in her bag, but decided to let him be the hunter.

'Excellent. I'll have ham.'

He returned almost immediately.

'They won't take cards. You have any Euros at all?'

'Just six.'

'We can share a sandwich.'

Twenty minutes later:

'Cafe was out of food, can you believe it? Stood in the queue for ages, then she says: No. Food.' His face was childishly righteous.

'Stop laughing. Did you hear me? Not a sausage! They run an airport that can't cater!'

'How about the paper shop?' she asked, swallowing her giggles.

'Not a single sweet left. Not even a bag of crisps. Condoms and cigarettes, that's your lot.'

'Oh dear.'

She got out her cheese sandwiches. Silently handed one to him, and he began eating without looking at her. She ate too, and then they drank from the bottle of water she'd brought, but just a little. They were stuck in a foreign airport with no money, no food, no other water and no departure time. And the toilets – well! He screwed the top back on the bottle, seemed weirdly at peace. Sighed, stretched. Looked at his watch.

'Bloody hell.'

'What?'

'It's almost ten o'clock.'

'Goodness. Isn't time behaving strangely? Last I looked, which feels half an hour ago, it was seven thirty.'

Her voice was odd, and he looked at her sharply.

'Well, it is, isn't it? Time is strange. It's the strangest thing there is.' She returned his sharp stare with one of her own. Their old combative stance, eyebrows cocked. He yawned suddenly, and a second later, she did too, turning away from him. Her eyes scanned the floor for a good sleeping place. Right here, with the seats above them? Floor space was rapidly disappearing. The floor near the walls was emerging as desirable real estate.

The lights dimmed. After a pause, people tried to do what they normally did. Teeth were brushed publicly and toothpaste swallowed not spit. Children were put in makeshift pyjamas; teddies were found and stories read. Women smeared night cream on their faces, and men were surprised to see women who were not their wives, behave exactly as their own wives behaved. Beds and pillows were made from towels, jumpers, t-shirts.

Joanna and George arranged their belongings closely around them, slipped their money and passports into pillows made from t-shirts stuffed with other t-shirts, and lowered their bodies to the dirty marble floor. They covered themselves with cardigans and beach towels. At first it felt ridiculous; they felt wide awake and silly. Look at them, on the very floor they'd been walking on all day! But soon, it felt normal. As if they'd been refugees for years.

George's last words were: 'Never again. You can go on your own next time, I'll be happy staying home with the dogs. And the sheep. And the rain. You know where you are with dogs and sheep and rain.'

'I love you,' she replied after a few minutes, but he didn't answer. She wondered if she'd spoken out loud. Then she wondered if she was a ghost. Drowned in the Mediterranean, and that was why he couldn't hear her. In a mild panic, she reviewed the previous hours for proof she was indeed not dead.

She remembered sleeping rough when she was eighteen, hitchhiking everywhere. This same good kind of tiredness, a certain looseness of limbs. Falling asleep in strange places – train stations, vineyards, building sites, beaches. Trusting the world enough to slide into sleep, no matter where she was. She'd forgotten that part of being young; that part of her self. She'd forgotten this way of living, stripping everything down to its bare bones. How liberating to pass a night without a bed, without a room, without light. Night was just a chunk of time to get through, like any other. Then the momentum of her long day took over, and she felt a delicious tingling creep over her skin.

It turned out that no matter where they were, they still spooned into each other. Her arm hooked round his belly, and her face nuzzled into his broad back. Around them lay several hundred bodies also abandoned to slumber; snoring, farting, twitching in dreams. Once she woke briefly and noticed airport staff cruising the terminal silently, like they were in a hospital, or a warehouse pumped full of sleeping gas. Around her, everybody slept except the Russian man who'd been a beautiful boy. She fell asleep again, listening to him. He ranted and ranted, but softly, considerately. As if singing a lullaby.'

Gorgeous

Robert James Berry

It's gorgeously cold
the rats smell sweet
the brown rice steams
the lentils reek.

Inhale this
big ladle of poverty
and happiness
crunch on your lollipop
stick out a purple tongue.

Early Days

Harry Giles

work as if you live in the early days of a better nation
shirk as if you live in the early days of a better vacation
lurk as if you live in the early days of a better mission
irk as if you live in the early days of a better sedition
smirk as if you live in the early days of a better notion
perk as if you live in the early days of a better potion
jerk as if you live in the early days of a better lotion
twerk as if you live in the early days of a better motion

Pathways of the mind

Doubling Back
Linda Cracknell

Freight Books, RRP £14.99, 256pp

Linda Cracknell's *Doubling Back* is the story of "ten paths trodden in memory". The dual meaning of the subtitle is deliberate – some of the walks are routes Cracknell took in her youth while others are paths taken by those no longer with her, including her father, a keen mountaineer who died young. Whether strolling through the Cornish countryside or clinging to Alpine peaks, the book is about the connections between landscape, memory and identity.

Cracknell's prose has always had a strong sense of place, from the harsh wilderness of the Caithness coastline in *Call of the Undertow* to hot muggy gardens in *The Searching Glance,* but in *Doubling Back* nature is no longer in service to the story. It is the story. As a reader of her work for years I could immediately tell there was something different about this book. Cracknell was clearly in familiar, comfortable territory, even while recounting times when she was physically far out of her comfort zone. There is the sense of a writer stretching into full suppleness, much the way a hiker does in the first few miles. There's deep and subtle skill here. The reader can relax and trust the guide.

Many of these walks are done in groups, some alongside animals, while a few are solo missions. In each case the preoccupation is the relationship between the walker and the environment. As her mind skips from topic to topic, in one paragraph running from walking to Obama to a favourite library in Scotland to writing, her feet beat the path and it's not long before the mountains and valleys are central again. Many writers of this kind of creative non-fiction live and write for the encounters with people, other walkers, locals and there are enlightening scenes with Kenyan women and Spanish olive grove workers, but this is a book for those of us who are secretly more alive when left to our own thoughts. Cracknell greets these people, is happy to see them but is soon on the path once more, interaction a break from the real journey. "Dialogue pattered on in my head... between my feet and the land... to me, not walking and not ever being alone would be to deny a part of myself."

The routes taken, beginning with retracing her own teenage steps in Cornwall and ending with a familiar walk near her home in Aberfeldy, don't just introduce us to a disparate variety of locales – Kenya, Spain, Switzerland, Norway – but build up a picture of the writer as a person. We are the sum total of the journeys we have taken and *Doubling Back* illustrates this perfectly. While walking a drovers' track on Rannoch Moor for the first time, she comes across paths she walked years earlier, skirting a mountain she climbed with friends, the world at once familiar and unfamiliar. The places, the people, the influences are all connected through Cracknell. Thomas Hardy and Jessie Kesson, Arabic plumbing, a man escaping from the Nazis in 1944. These walks and these stories form a biography, a memoir with her at the centre connecting everything.

Then there are the paths not taken. Ever present is the father she tragically never met and the relationship that only existed through photos and accounts of his own mountaineering exploits. There are ghosts aplenty in the hills, figures from history, much loved writers, ex-partners and unborn children.

Because of this, *Doubling Back* becomes much more than a travel book, a book about walking and climbing. It's a deeply moving examination of why we scale dangerous peaks and lose ourselves in desolate wilderness, why we squelch through peat bogs and move through the world with nothing but what we can carry. It's the story of how all this movement is life, how these journeys create us. Humanity is perpetually in movement but sometimes we have to be alone, battered by wind and rain on a road used for centuries before we realise the deep connections we have with history. We don't scale mountains because they are there, we do it because we are.

— *Peekachoo*

Modern Morality Tale

The Last Treasure Hunt
Jane Alexander

Saraband, RRP £8.99, 320pp

Campbell Johnstone is thirty and going nowhere fast, stuck behind a Glasgow bar while his friends mature and move on. A novel about a close-knit group of pals and cousins from Perthshire, the dynamics of their relationships and the inevitable civil war may seem at first glance very 'debut Scottish novel', but *The Last Treasure Hunt* quickly asserts itself as something unique, and a timely publication.

One of the childhood friends, Eve Sadler, is The Next Big Thing, a young, beautiful actress with a string of successful Hollywood supporting roles, back in Scotland to film her first lead alongside Morgan Freeman. When they were kids Eve, a few years younger than the others, worshipped Campbell and followed him around. Campbell spent most of his time trying to ditch her, yet now, drawn by Eve's new-found glamour and with after-images of a particularly memorable sex scene in one of her early films, Campbell sneaks on set and tries to renew the friendship. Needless to say, it all goes wrong.

The Last Treasure Hunt is a modern morality tale. Campbell is quickly caught up in a world of paparazzi, showbiz agents and exclusive parties and he falls hard for the modern Faustian pact – fame in return for your soul. He moves to London, splashes money around like it has a use-by date and falls for his own hype. The more stories about Eve he sells, the more soap starlets he's snapped with, the more his friends distance themselves from him. Aware that his fame is borrowed from Eve, he attempts to prove himself in his own right with predictable car-crash results. The media know the script. The press giveth and the press taketh away: he's heading for a very public fall and when it comes, it's front page news.

An early scene sets up the heart of the novel: Campbell is alone in his flat Googling pictures of Eve and reading 'Starspotter' sightings. There's a disconnect. Eve on screen, Eve on Google is not the Eve he grew up with. She's a celebrity. To us, celebrities aren't real people. Later on, when he's mulling a one-night stand with a fellow D-lister, delighted that it's made the tabloids, we get the second part of the argument – to men, women aren't real people. Throughout the book Campbell is casually, subconsciously misogynistic. Following those premises, his actions are justified. That's the world we live in.

This is why, perhaps more than the excellent analysis of the modern media and the control it has over those caught in its net, *The Last Treasure Hunt* is a timely book. In an age of internet trolls, slut-shaming and online rape threats, a dialogue has begun about the experiences of famous women and the treatment all women receive from men. Campbell is symbolic of both. Not a bad guy, he's just naïve and unthinkingly selfish. Alexander is too subtle to slap this message across the pages but it infuses

every sentence, and structures the novel – if Campbell stopped for one moment and exercised an iota of empathy, he could avoid the impending crash. Of course, he never does. *The Last Treasure Hunt* is a masterclass on what happens when empathy is absent.

Alexander handles Campbell's naïvety and self-delusion well. Writing from the point of view of someone lying to themselves is a tricky balancing act but one she deftly pulls off. By the time Campbell realises what the reader has known all along, it's too late and he slinks home for the dramatic dénouement.

Jane Alexander has won prizes for her short stories, and her debut novel marks the arrival of an important new voice.

— *Totoro*

Talking Across

Infidelities
Kirsty Gunn

Faber and Faber, RRP £12.99, 224pp

Kirsty Gunn introduces *Infidelities*, her collection of short stories, with a teasing vignette that appears autobiographical, about a writer who has just finished writing a short-story collection called *Infidelities*. The writer says of her stories, 'I'm not discovering the story, and then writing it down. No. From the beginning, I was there […] I'm in the midst.' So, as I begin to read, I'm looking for her. Where is she, this writer who has just described kissing her ex, at a late hour when her children and husband are asleep, and who seems to be implying that the book I'm about to read is dangerously confessional?

At first she does a good job of hiding; she is a perfect ventriloquist. Each story has a distinct voice with it's own dialect and syntax, each voice at one with the story's preoccupations and the character's state of mind. 'Listen to me now, you. How I sound.' One character vocalises this, but every story in the collection demands it.

The first, 'A Story She Might Tell Herself', slows me right down. It keeps taking asides into seemingly inconsequential details, the details that the protagonist Helen's life is composed of. I'm not immediately disposed to appreciate this, because of course the other thing I'm looking for is infidelity. The collection's title and introduction have primed me for a juicy exposé. So I reconcile myself to the idea that this is a book for a patient reader, and I settle down to read each sentence with restful attention, letting the details accrete to the tidal turn of the story.

My expectations are thrown again by 'The Scenario', the third story in the collection. The playful meta-fiction of the introduction is back with a vengeance. It's a story about someone writing a story about someone telling a story. Or is it a story about a conversation about someone writing a story about someone telling a story? These layers intersect surprisingly and amusingly as the characters flirt with each other and the story flirts with ideas about 'meaning and perception, language and the body,' and

'high, high theory.'

The structure of the book places all these voices in relation to each other. In the introduction, a conversation between the writer and her ex inspires the three sections of the book, 'Going Out', 'Staying Out', and 'Never Coming Home'. It also mentions the final story, 'Infidelity', so that a thread of curiosity runs through the book and the end links back nicely to the beginning.

'Infidelity' has the satisfying effect of acting as a commentary on the rest of the collection as Gunn examines, with playful irony, the process of writing a short story. Helen, the writer in the story, tries to follow her tutor's instructions, but she is beset with doubts, second guessing herself, worrying about the experience of the reader and how to fictionalise reality. She also worries about the title of her story, and whether she can meet the expectations it sets up.

So here the writer is again, I've found her. Of course she gradually emerges in the other stories, or perhaps more correctly, between them, because despite their different voices they talk to each other across the collection. They talk about women and children working out who they are, in relation to their husbands, fathers, families; they talk about storytelling; they talk about how peoples' lives change due to tiny consequential details. They also talk about infidelity and how it can be a kiss, a telephone call, letting go of a memory, or just a feeling.

— *Héloïse*

A Difficult Reward

The Surfacing
Cormac James

Sandstone Press, RRP £8.99, 382pp

In 1845 an entire expedition of over a hundred men led by Sir John Franklin simply disappeared in their attempt to find a way from the Atlantic to the Pacific through the fabled 'North West Passage' in the Arctic reaches of Canada. The fate of the Franklin expedition, which is the context of 'The Surfacing', still has the power to generate not only fiction but also headlines; the first of the two ships belonging to this expedition was located just a few months ago. And in general, accounts of polar exploration continue to both fascinate and appall us. In our era of continuous surveillance and communication, these experiences of years of isolation and hardship can feel as psychologically remote to us as descriptions of medieval warfare.

'The Surfacing' ostensibly follows the fortunes of one of several expeditions who were launched to discover what had happened to Franklin and his men. The story is told from the point of view of Morgan, the second-in-command on 'The Impetus'. When the ship stops off en route at a small village in Greenland and Morgan makes the acquaintance of Kitty, a Danish woman living there, the reader can easily anticipate the conflict that will arise as a result of her later discovered on board, pregnant with Morgan's child.

But the book disdains the obvious route. The stowaway is accepted, almost as a matter of course, and the fact that she is pregnant seems to be welcomed. The officers and men look after her, they make her furniture and she gets a warm cabin to herself. Only Morgan feels any psychological discomfort, but that is clearly secondary to the main problem of how to make progress in the hostile polar environment. Very soon the boat is trapped in the rapidly growing sea ice and Morgan finds himself in command.

The real conflict is in the mind – what is the best course of action? Should they abandon the boat and sledge to the nearest settlement, risking death by hypothermia in the snow and ice? Or should they stay on board and possibly starve to death? These are problems that can be considered by the application of logic, and by using experience gleaned from previous expeditions. But nothing prepares Morgan for what happens to him when the baby is born, and that is the true theme of the book.

Like the men in the ship, the reader feels marooned in this novel. The context fades away, the fate of Franklin is hardly ever discussed. People's former lives are rarely referred to, letters from home aren't particularly welcomed and the reason for Kitty deciding to abandon her former life is never fully explored. This claustrophobia reinforces the fact that the only reality that matters to anyone on board is the situation they find themselves in. Because of the way that the plot closes down to focus on the immediate circumstances the reader is forced to share that isolation. And this claustrophobia is underlined by the sharp and cold intensity of the language, which feels as if it's stripped back to the essentials. Reading this book is frequently, and presumably deliberately, disorientating and it can sometimes be tricky to figure out what is going on. But it achieves a hard-won emotional punch in its descriptions of Morgan falling in love with his son, and finally understanding the point of life as he faces death. James, overall, offers a difficult but rewarding read.

— *Bear of Little Brain*

Restless Flight

The Drum Tower
by Farnoosh Moshiri

Sandstone, RRP £8.99, 308pp

Set against the backdrop of the Iranian Revolution in 1979, *The Drum Tower* is Farnoosh Moshiri's fourth novel, told through the eyes of sixteen-year-old Talkhoon and capturing the political unease and disorder of the time.

Talkhoon lives in the centre of Tehran in Drum Tower; a house haunted by the ghosts of absent loved ones and family secrets. Here, Talkhoon lives with her grandfather Baba-Ji – who spends his days obsessively writing a book about the Simorgh, the legendary Bird of Knowledge – and a bitter unloving grandmother, Khanum-Jaan, who reserves her affection for Talkhoon's beautiful sister, Taara. After

Talkhoon's failed suicide attempt, Khanum-Jaan banishes her to the basement of Drum Tower, leaving her at the mercy of the unwelcome advances of the sinister 'Uncle' Assad.

Talkhoon is a neglected child, struggling to comprehend the mysterious absence of her mother and the abandonment of her father, a political rebel on the run. Talkhoon's grief deepens when her beloved grandfather falls into a coma, leaving the epic story of the Simorgh bird incomplete. The personal letters of Khanum-Jaan to her late father provide a break in Talkhoon's narrative, and act as a tool to reveal deep rooted family secrets, also providing the reader with a deepening insight into Khanum-Jaan's loveless marriage and her own sense of abandonment.

Trapped within a family of self-absorbed eccentrics, Talkhoon is one of the few characters within this novel who evokes sympathy and the reader is soon rooting for her escape. The story opens with Talkhoon describing herself as 'crazy', her head full of the 'screams of the wind', but we soon understand that her grandmother has contributed greatly to this self perception, and Talkhoon is probably the sanest of them all.

After a bit of a slow start, the narrative pace picks up when Talkhoon begins to plot her escape. By Part III, the reader is fully absorbed in Talkhoon's journey towards the Afghanistan border, heart beating along with hers at every step. The threat of Assad's occupation of Drum Tower, and growing advances to Talkhoon herself, adds to the tension and urgency of her getaway.

The darkness of Talkhoon's situation and the themes of the novel are lightened by Moshiri's lyrical and descriptive prose. Lines such as, 'The scent of all the grasses of the world, of long forgotten springs, of unknown and nameless wild flowers filled the room', add a sensual richness to Talkhoon's surroundings. Moshiri is skilled in bringing all things to life, with the Drum House itself becoming a character, and even the parrot Boor-boor and dog, Jhangi, developing rounded personalities along with the other occupants. Moshiri has the ability to weave in the political issues of the time, without making it just a novel about politics. Talkhoon's story is one of loss and isolation, but also courage and the pursuit of personal freedom – not just from the oppression of the rising unease within Iran, but from the prison in which her family have encased her.

The image of the Simorgh bird provides a symbol of freedom throughout the novel, slightly tainted by the recurring description of the tattooed version on Assad's stomach. This almost ruins the beauty of the bird, but perhaps serves as an important reminder that most of the characters hold the image of the bird within their minds as a symbol of hope and survival. For me, Talkhoon is the bird – a delicate girl who grows in strength and bravery in order to fly from the cage of Drum Tower.

— *Anansie*

Spirit Words

The Book of Ways
Colin Will

Red Squirrel Press, RRP £8.99, 240pp

In his new collection, *The Book of Ways*, Colin Will defines the Japanese form of haibun as 'sketching in words', and as 'prose written in the spirit of haiku'; which usually contains a haiku as a conclusion. It is also a journey, whether literal, metaphorical or both.

The book, at first glance, looks more like prose, being novel length at more than 200 pages; and the haibun itself seems too prosey. But after a few pages, one soon eases into the meditative pace, and the poetry quickly emerges. Highlights include some of Will's travels through Europe, North America and Japan; his fear of heights; a fear of dying (but not of death); and memories of his childhood in Edinburgh:

"One of my teachers, and I forget how old I was when I met him, was Mr MacCaig. That's how we knew him. Norman came much later."

The writing is richly textured and deeply personal, without being banal. It celebrates the extraordinary in the ordinary, honing in on key moments – often using sensory detail – that colour a place or experience with its own particular mood. The reader delights in the simple joy Will recounts upon harvesting vegetables from his allotment; and there are well-wrought details of food from around the world, which often transcend their physical locations. He recounts a restaurant in Hungary, for example:

> "Czardaš with your goulash, sir?
>
> the old Red poet
> spoke up for old tyrannies
> from his Brownsbank home"

What makes the haiku seem stronger is the immediacy of understanding when reading; whereas the haibun comprise more of a meandering journey, which the haiku encapsulates at the end of each passage. It is impressive that he wrote the entire book during a four-week Hawthornden residency (with or without notes or a plan, it is not known). This is a book to savour slowly, like

> "a glass of whisky
> with a wee drop of water
> at the day's ending."

— *The Waxwing Slain*

What, no angst?

The Space Between: New and Selected Poems
Sheena Blackhall

Publisher, RRP £16.99, 166pp

Sheena Blackhall is simply not playing by the rules. She shows no respect for the conventions of modern literature: spurning the well-recognised boundary, for example, between poetry and songs. For years now she has been completely disregarding the etiquette of publishing meagre books of verse at irregular, and preferably long, intervals: she is outrageously prolific, having produced one hundred volumes. One hundred! That's more than the rest of us Scottish poets put together! Not only that, but she seems to think that it is reasonable to write in two different languages, and to be funny. I bet she doesn't live in a garret either.

In this new book, lavishly produced by Aberdeen University Press, we get a snapshot of what she has been up to. And what variety! How dare she? The poems span almost the full range of what it is legitimate to call a poem, from tiny couplets and haiku through sonnets to multi-page ballads from the same fireside as Robbie Burns. Many of them are in Doric, appropriate for the Makar of Aberdeen, including possibly the bawdiest poem I have ever read, the hilarious 'Heich Fur Houghmagandie', from which I almost dare not quote for fear of shocking upstanding readers. Suffice it to say that when "the

Spurtle bangs the coggie", there is more than porridge being made.

Don't be put off by the Doric. The poems communicate directly; they say it straight and true, which is not to imply that they aren't clever. Sheena Blackhall is a master of form and a virtuoso player with metre and rhyme, and it is as if she has worked hard so that we don't need to do anything but revel in the wordplay. Here's her portrait of Allt Darrarie – Burn of the Stunning Noise – Glen Muick:

"Slaverin, slubberin, gibberin,
          gabberin,
Roon wi a wallop, a sklyter, a sweel,
Yonder's the burn – in its bairnhood,
          it's blabberin –
Heich-lowpin puddock, wi virr in its
          heel."

You simply don't need to know every word to love the music of it and get the drift.

If I am allowed one gripe with the book it is with the glossary. It includes words that don't need to be there (splurge, tatties, cairn) yet omitting a great many words the reader needs to know, including kyte, scurl, lave, screivin, winnlestrae and even houghmagandie!

The poetry itself, though, is a delight. There are laugh-out-loud daft poems (you can imagine what is 'In a Handbag, Darkly'), deeply philosophical poems, verse for children, lists, elegies, wedding poems, satire and translations into Scots of a wide range of writers from ancient oriental poets, to Rumi, Milosz and John Clare. Many of the poems are about nature. I particularly enjoyed 'Bat': "Poor pipistrelle, in your pauper's membrane, / wafer-thin as gauze... the huddled wings / Coiffing the small collapse of your /Smokey, ash-bud face.. Your brothers are swooping, fat, / In moon-milk lappings of flight!"

Sheena Blackhall's poetry is always sharp and often witty whichever language she's using. One English poem, 'In the Interests of Democracy', advocates a flat earth, while 'The Yird' makes the wish come true, in Doric. This is a poet who breaks all the rules, even, it seems, the laws of physics.

"Fin aabody kent the Yird was flat
As a Japanee Chinee plate
Ye cud gyang frae snaw in an Arctic
          floe
Tae a desert bi roller skate
Bit near the edge far Space began.
Wis fu o haar an dim
Sae gin ye traivelled frae here tae there
Ye tae slow doon near the rim."

— *Count Duckula*

Increasingly Cold

Cold City
Cathy McSporran

Freight Books, RRP £8.99, 320pp

There are just not enough great Glasgow novels. In perhaps the greatest of them all, Alasdair Gray's *Lanark*, the characters McAlpin and Duncan Thaw discuss why this may be, "Glasgow is a magnificent city," said McAlpin. "Why do we hardly ever notice that?" "Because nobody imagines living here […] if a city hasn't been used by an artist, not even the inhabitants live there imaginatively." If this is the case, any new imagining of Glasgow is to be celebrated. Cathy McSporran's novel *Cold City* is just that, and while it is not one of those great novels, there is enough style and innovation to suggest that this is a writer of great promise.

The novel opens with Susan Pherson spotting her recently deceased Dad walking on Argyle Street before seeing him entering a building which doesn't exist. At the time she believes she has seen into a different world. In the following days she feels increasingly cold, unable to find any heat in the city. She cannot even take comfort in sleep, and her situation leads to her taking drastic measures as she becomes desperate for some relief.

When she wakes from a period of unconsciousness she finds herself in another Glasgow, one which is familiar, but where her nearest and dearest have led slightly different lives to those she knows, and, to them, she has unexpectedly returned from the dead. With echoes of the aforementioned 'Lanark', as well as Iain Banks' 'The Bridge', Susan finds herself waking alternatively in one of two alternate realities, one where she is being monitored in hospital, under a regime of drugs and psychotherapy, and the other which is increasingly more appealing to her, despite the city being constantly in deep freeze.

It is when she travels between these two worlds that the novel is at its most appealing and unexpected as the reader, like Susan, is never sure where she is going to find herself. Both 'Glasgows' are wonderfully portrayed with just enough detail and difference to make them both believable. When Susan walks the streets it fulfils Gray's wish that the city should be portrayed imaginatively, and you can feel the chill coming off the page. It is when the novel moves events out of the city to the Scottish Highlands that it becomes less engaging, although never less than interesting, but not always for the right reasons.

It is here that Susan confronts charismatic and creepy Christian fundamentalist leader, McLean, and the novel changes pace and tone, which is not purely down to the change of location and terrain. The 'trips' to hospital almost stop altogether, and what began as a curious, supernatural, tale, almost a Glasgow ghost story, becomes something closer to a political thriller, which I found more than a little jarring.

Cold City is a thought provoking novel, but I was so impressed with the first two thirds that I couldn't help but be disappointed as it drew to a close. McSporran's ambition is impressive, but in the end I found the novel takes on too much. It touches on alternate realities, religion, paganism, philosophy, Norse mythology, psychoanalysis, sexual identity, grief, politics and much more. The best novels usually demand work from readers, but in this instance there are too many times when the enquiries lead to dead ends.

Don't misunderstand me, 'Cold City' is a remarkable novel in many ways, but loses its focus and clarity towards the end in a manner that almost negates the initial enjoyment, and that is more frustrating than reading a novel that is simply, consistently, OK.

— *Kes*

Same Strange Place

New Publications from Happenstance Press.

Ruthven Todd's pamphlet,
The Ghost of Dylan Thomas,
RRP £3.60 32pp

Tom Cleary's pamphlet,
The Third Miss Keane,
RRP £4.00, 28pp

Richard Osmond's pamphlets
Shill and *Variant Air*
RRP £4.00, 28pp

Tom Duddy's second collection,
The Years, RRP £12, 80 pp

Ruthven Todd's pamphlet *The Ghost of Dylan Thomas* presents itself as an explanation for why Todd's biography of the poet was never written. It reflects on the impossibility of reducing complex humanity to prose, and how the accumulation of data on someone departed – conflicting testimonies, memories, judgements – can occlude the friend lost and haunt the compiler. Although it's concerned with Thomas's legacy, at the heart of this book is an account of a warm friendship with Dylan Thomas the man, rather than the poet. As such, it's unexpectedly moving, worthy of a wider readership than first appearances may suggest.

Tom Cleary's pamphlet *The Third Miss Keane* is in form and presentation a poetry collection, but the back-cover describes the author as 'a born story-teller', pointing to the realisation that these poems are more akin to extremely compressed, unsettling short stories. They recall most strongly the adult work of Roald Dahl. Like Dahl's *Tales of The Unexpected*, the poems twist in the closing lines, with a strong narrative push leading to the conclusion. That's not to suggest that they fail as verse – they are constructed with attention to economy and form. Horrors are suggested by the placing of a line break, and images linger past the closing couplet.

This episodic format helps the collection cohere. It feels as if the world where "Matty lived for a whole year / in a hardwood and glass hut on the lawn" ('Matty') is the same one in which "The wheelbarrow people had a god who lived behind a wall" and "James would soon be required to kill his father," ('The Wheelbarrow People') like they are all vignettes of the same, strange place. All in all it's a very pleasing debut.

Richard Osmond has published two

pamphlets concurrently, each appearing to be the work of a different poet. One, 'Shill,' is modern, with references to 1980s horror films and Aphex Twin; the second, 'Variant Air,' is inspired by and apes Gerard Manley Hopkins – its centrepiece poem, 'The Fire in The Cottonian Library,' both memorialises the fire that damaged the Beowulf manuscript along with other Old English texts and is explicitly inspired by Hopkins' 'The Wreck of The Deutschland.' It's a great deal of weight for one poem to bear, and it inevitably suffers for it. Osmond is clearly a talented poet, but the presentation makes a comparison with Hopkins unavoidable, and it's a comparison that hurts Osmond.

That said, Hopkins could never have written *Shill*, which is playful, funny and unserious in the best way. If there is a complaint, it's that it's possibly too slight in places, just as *Variant Air* feels too stuffy sometimes. If Osmond can achieve a synthesis of these different styles, there may be a great single collection forthcoming.

The jacket of Tom Duddy's *The Years* tells me it was assembled posthumously, and a sense of this mortality runs through the pages. The poems are conversational, direct. The epithet 'story-teller' is again, accurately, applied by the jacket, but unlike Cleary's tight, enclosed poems, these works are open-ended and sparkle with warmth. Is it fanciful to think that the knowledge that this is his last collection, knowing that Duddy knew this was a capstone of sorts, colours the reading of a collection? No, but these poems are strong enough to stand apart from external biography. They

are beautiful and tender, and ultimately optimistic. The prevailing feeling is not regret and sadness at the closing of a life, but joy and thanks for a life that was full.

— *Sredni Vashtar*

Bringing About Change

New publications from Stewed Rhubarb Press.

Anne Connolly
Not Entirely Beautiful
RRP £5.00, 22pp

Russell Jones
Places of Their Own
RRP £5.00, 20pp

Ryan Van Winkle & Dan Gorman
ViewMaster
RRP £5.00, 14pp

Jo Clifford
The Gospel According to Jesus, Queen of Heaven
RRP £5.00, 27pp

stewedrhubarb.org

I've heard Anne Connolly perform her poems, and her pamphlet *Not Entirely Beautiful* serves to underscore my impression of Connolly as a poet operating fruitfully on the interstice between poetry for the page and poetry for performance. There are concrete poems such as 'Preview' with its gravid curve on the page to powerful poems that you find yourself reading aloud, such as 'A Kind of Dancing' where a knee-capped victim of the Troubles dances in the refrains of a poem about the long haul towards peace. There is a trenchant playfulness on offer here, such as the witty poem 'Bee Division' where the life of the hive is extended allegorically to the serving and ruling classes in society.

Russell Jones's *Spaces of Their Own* is a much more outré, sci-fi affair. There are elements of the playfulness of Edwin Morgan's space and concrete poems on which Jones based his PhD thesis, such as 'Teleportation Error' which seems based on Morgan's 'Message Clear'. Also 'The Bang' (a conversation between two opposing protons in the Large Hadron Collider) owes a debt to Morgan's 'Gorgo and Beau'. However, on a few occasions I was convinced this was more than outer-space fun and games. 'After the Moons' offers a chilling, utilitarian view of human survival in the space age and other poems like 'Blue Planet' seem to undermine our safe assumptions about the security of the world in which we live:

"(...) On Earth we are the mine,
the miner, pickaxe and cutter,
expert, assessor. We are the jewellers

That emerald glow might weep us
up like a grainy imperfection (...)"

Ryan Van Winkle and Dan Gorman's joint sound and poetry work *ViewMaster* is often meditative and haunting. Some of these poems seem inspired by lines of Sufi wisdom or the divan of Hafiz twinned with the lightness and lift of Frank O'Hara and the New York school:

"Son, any dream can be a river
any river a way of life what else
can you want from a world?
Drum on the rocks and don't ask
where she comes from / where she goes
kiss her – for now, she is here."

I'd say more than any other pamphlet here, *ViewMaster* needs to be read as well as listened to, as these poems come to life aurally with Van Winkle's rhythmic readings and Gorman's ambient sound work around each poem. Together they produce emotive and sonic landscapes as worthy of any 'viewmaster'.

Jo Clifford's verse play *The Gospel According to Jesus, Queen of Heaven* is easily the most important work discussed here, a deeply necessary re-imagining of Jesus as a transgender 'Queen of Heaven'. Just as Dennis Potter caused religious uproar with his 1969 play *Son of Man*, which imagines Jesus fraught with human self-doubt as the son of God, Clifford's profoundly positive and humane play was judged by many Christians who had not seen nor read it before. I think the root of the controversy about this play is nothing to do with the fact that Jesus is transgender, but that Jesus is shown to not solely own the freehold on suffering and martyrdom. The crucifixion becomes an egalitarian concept in Clifford's play with LGBT people suffering daily at the hands of the intolerant: 'This is where we get crucified'. Clifford's vision is both forgiving and empowering:

"Bless you if people abuse you or persecute you
because it means you are bringing about change."

— *Black Sheep*

Dear Gutter

I'm a published writer but my partner shows no interest in my work. How can our relationship grow when she's not interested in participating in such an important aspect of my life?

I am a writer in my late thirties and recently published my first novel, fulfilling a long-held ambition. The book was well received and this has given me enough encouragement to believe it's worth attempting a career as an author. I currently have a full-time job but would love to go part-time at some point and, in my dreams, one day write full-time. During the four years it took to complete the novel, my wife was supportive, and I tried hard to minimise the impact on family life by writing late at night after everyone had gone to bed.

My problem is that she hasn't taken any pleasure in my moderate success. She seems genuinely uninterested in what I'm doing, doesn't want to come to literary events with me, had to be dragged to the book's launch, and although a reader, hasn't shown any interest in looking at any of the drafts or the final published book. I love my partner hugely but this ambivalence is very hurtful. We have two funny, noisy, beautiful children and share equally the majority of childcare. I feel I pull my weight as a husband and cannot help but see this lack of interest in something that is increasingly important to me as some kind of betrayal that could be devastating for our relationship.

Gutter says

You don't say how long you've been together but I'm guessing, by the reference to two kids, a minimum of five years and, more likely, a decade at least. There's nothing like children to give you and your wife a shared interest, a project in common, that helps cement your commitment to each other. While the patter of tiny feet can of course place a huge strain on a relationship, I'm a great believer that, if a couple works together, parenthood not only makes you both grow up – sometimes at different rates – but can also create a deeper connection than almost any other experience. Sharing a child with someone establishes a bond that lasts a lifetime, whether we like it or not.

However, very few of us get all our fulfilment from being parents alone. And considering the blighters will leave home eventually, some sooner than others, it's advisable to have other interests in preparation for that eventuality. After the initial onslaught of broken sleep and stinking nappies, tantrums and hyperactivity – which, let's face it, can be tedious in the extreme – once we feel that we're on top of things, it's at that point that we start thinking about what else life holds.

I salute the energy and commitment that it took to write a book, particularly in the early years of fatherhood. That's an achievement. That you wrote a book that people like is an even greater success. Public praise from random strangers, whether on Amazon or in the press, delivers a highly addictive buzz. And now, understandably, you'd like some more.

The first question I'd suggest you ask yourself is did you discuss your plans to write with your wife before you started? You may have already been scribbling away when you first met but, considering the time, effort and concentration required to complete a novel, energy not directed at family life regardless of when you do it, she may well feel you're giving the best part of yourself to literature, not to her and your kids. Writers can be on another planet mid-novel. This could be causing great resentment which she doesn't feel she can express because she knows how important writing is to you.

If you've already floated the idea of going part-time, this may have set off alarm bells that she's going to have to pick up the financial slack while you chase rainbows. She may not regard writing as a legitimate job for a grown adult. Many don't. Anger can also build when we can see our partner consciously or unconsciously choosing a path that leads them away from us, reducing intimacy not increasing it. Writing is something she perhaps feels that she can't participate in, that it's a solo and thereby deeply selfish activity, which of course it is. For those with the impulse to write it's as natural as sleeping and eating, while for others it must appear supremely arrogant, thinking that the world should listen to us.

However, you should also consider the possibility that your wife may not actually like your work. Taste varies hugely and what works for one reader can drive another to distraction. She may have sneaked a peek at your novel and hated it. Meanwhile, her reluctance to go to literary events could be because she feels excluded from the club, or it may be a simple as a dislike for writers. We are a self-obsessed, needy bunch.

Many of us write partly for the validation and if that isn't forthcoming from our significant other it can be crushing. We only have one life. If you are seriously considering dedicating a large part of it to words, and if your partner doesn't regard that as worthwhile, then a wedge will be driven between you. The most important thing to do is of talk to each other. When you've peace and quiet and there aren't distractions that allow for evasion, discuss it frankly. Tell your partner how you feel but don't be defensive. Ask her how she feels. Make sure she knows it's safe for her to be honest. Ask her what she wants to achieve beyond parenthood. You may be surprised at her answer.

However, also consider just how important writing is to you. Would you be willing to give it up for her if she asked? If the answer is yes, then that may be all she needs to feel part of your choices. If the answer is no, then you need to be honest with her about the changing terms of your partnership. I bet it's not what she signed up for.

If you have a problem you'd like advice on send it to *deargutter@gmail.com*

Contributor Biographies

Rizwan Akhtar teaches at Department of English, Punjab University, Lahore, Pakistan. His poems have appeared in various publications including *Scottish Pen* and *Gutter*.

Kirstie Allan – scottish. poet. essayist. tusitala. maker. art criticism. wanderer. rambler. observer. **wee-poet.tumblr.com**

Rachelle Atalla is an Aberdeen based writer who has received a 2015 New Writers Award from the Scottish Book Trust.

Fran Baillie – Notebooks, bus tickets, receipts, scraps of paper smothered in words. This is life now that she's found POETRY! Yippee!

Jonathan Bay is a homegrown California transman who hopped the pond for education. He currently lives in Edinburgh.

Robert James Berry lives and writes in Dunedin, New Zealand. His poetry has been published widely. His ninth collection *Toffee Apples* is out now from Ginninderra Press, Adelaide, Australia.

William Bonar – shortlisted for 2015 New Writers Awards, his collection *Offering* will be published by Red Squirrel Press on 23rd April 2015.

Mark Buckland is the former publisher at Cargo. He now works in TV. This is his first published story in seven years.

Aimee Campbell lives in Glasgow. As well as working full-time, she makes wee animations and writes short stories.

Jim Carruth is the current Poet Laureate of Glasgow and his first full collection *Killochries* will be published by Freight in April 2015.

Nabin Kumar Chhetri is a final year student of a Masters Degree in Creative writing at the University of Oxford.

Defne Çizakça is a creative writing PhD candidate at the University of Glasgow in Scotland where she is working on a historical novel about 19th century Istanbul.

Zoe Coutts is 22 years old and studying English with Creative Writing on a merit scholarship at the University of Aberdeen

David Crystal was born in Prudhoe, Northumberland in 1963 and now lives and works in London. He has had two previous collections from Two Rivers Press. *Wrong Horse Home,* his last collection is available from TALL LIGHTHOUSE.

R.A. Davis was born in Edinburgh in 1983. He grew up in Kent and North Wales and belongs to Glasgow.

Cheryl Follon has published two poetry collections – *Dirty Looks* and *All Your Talk* – both with Bloodaxe Books.

Graham Fulton's latest collection is *Photographing Ghosts* (Roncadora Press). Two new books forthcoming from Red Squirrel Press and Salmon Poetry.

Janice Galloway is one of the UK's most versatile and gifted writers, author of novels, short stories, non-fiction, collaborative works with visual artists and musicians, operatic libretti and prose-poetry.

Harry Giles is a performer, poet, and general doer of things. He grew up in Orkney, Scotland, and now live in Edinburgh.

Marjorie Lotfi Gill is the Poet in Residence at Jupiter Artland and her poems have been published by *Ambit*, *Magma*, *Mslexia*, *The North* and *Rattle*.

Lesley Glaister has written thirteen novels, and currently teaches Creative Writing at the University of St Andrews. She lives in Edinburgh.

Danni Glover is a Glaswegian writer currently undertaking a PhD in Northern Ireland. She can be found at **danniglover.com**

Alasdair Gray Describing himself as a 'maker of imagined objects,' Alasdair Gray has been a prolific producer of novels, short stories, plays, poems, pamphlets and literary criticism.

Jennifer Morag Henderson is a writer from Inverness. Her biography of Josephine Tey will be published by Sandstone this autumn.

Diana Hendry's latest publication is *The Seed-Box Lantern: New & Selected Poems*. She's currently co-editor of *New Writing Scotland*.

Andy Jackson is editor of several poetry anthologies, the most recent being Double Bill. His new collection *A Beginner's Guide To Cheating* is due in 2015 via Red Squirrel Press.

Brian Johnstone's current collection is *Dry Stone Work* (Arc, 2014). His work appears on The Poetry Archive website later this year. **brianjohnstonepoet.co.uk**

Tareq al-Karmy is a Palestinian poet and activist from the West Bank. His poems appeared in Palestinian anthology *A Bird Is Not a Stone*.

Rached Khalifa is a Tunisian fiction writer in his debut. He also teaches literature at the University of Tunis. He is a greater lover of Scotland and things Scottish.

Dorothy Lawrenson Born in Dundee, Dorothy Lawrenson is a poet, artist and graphic designer. She is currently undertaking an MFA in Poetry at Texas State University.

William Letford has an M.Litt in Creative Writing from the University of Glasgow. His first collection, *Bevel*, was published by Carcanet Press in 2012.

Pippa Little is the recipient many awards and prizes, and her work has been widely published. Her latest collection, *Overwintering* (Oxford Poets), was released in 2012.

Juliet Lovering is a fiction writer, part time lecturer and mum to three young kids. She lives in rural Aberdeenshire.

Martin MacIntyre is an award-winning author, poet and storyteller now living in Edinburgh. *Cala Bendita 's a Bheannachdan* his most recent work of fiction was shortlisted for The 2014 Saltire Society Literary Book of The Year.

Micaela Maftei and **Laura Tansley** have been collaborating since 2010, and their work together has appeared in the anthology *Tip Tap Flat* and *Kenyon Review Online*. They are co-editors of the forthcoming collection *Determining the Form: Writing Creative Non-Fiction*. They live and work in Victoria, B.C. and Glasgow, respectively.

Ian McPherson Winner of first Time Out Comedy Award. Author of *The Autobiography of Ireland's Greatest Living Genius*. Recently completed *The Book of Blaise*.

Joe McInnes has had short stories published in *Gutter* and *New Writing Scotland*. He is currently working on his first novel.

Hugh McMillan's selected poems will be out later this year along with the sublimely weird *Galloway: An Unreliable Tour*.

James McGonigal, poet and biographer, has edited Edwin Morgan's *The Midnight Letterbox: Selected Correspondence 1950–2010*, forthcoming from Carcanet Press.

Donald S Murray's latest book, *SY StorY* is published by Birlinn in February. His play *Sequamur* is being performed in various locations throughout Scotland in March.

Chris Powici lives in Dunblane, teaches creative writing for The Open University and The University of Stirling, and edits the literary magazine *Northwords Now*. A new collection of his poetry, *This Weight of Light*, is due to be published in May 2015.

Wayne Price's short stories and poems have won many awards. His first short story collection *Furnace* and his novel *Mercy Seat* are published by Freight Books.

Kay Ritchie, recently Clydebuilt, is published in *Tracks in the Sand*, *Shorelines*, *Black Middens*, *Glad Rag*, *Treasures*, *Making Waves* & *A Star in the Heart*.

Cynthia Rogerson writes mainstream literary fiction, set in Scotland and California. She is the author of four novels and one collection of short stories. Her stories have also appeared in numerous anthologies.

Stewart Sanderson is writing a PhD on modern Scots translation. Last year he was shortlisted for the Edwin Morgan Award.

Hamish Scott is originally from Edinburgh. His poetry has been published in various outlets and by The Laverock's Nest Press.

Roddy Shippin is a writer from Edinburgh. He helps run Blind Poetics and edit the poetry at *Valve Journal*.

Kathrine Sowerby lives in Glasgow where she runs Tell It Slant, a poetry bookshop, and makes the publication *fourfold*.

Gerda Stevenson regularly writes drama for radio. Her poetry and prose have been widely published in literary magazines, newspapers and anthologies throughout Britain and abroad.

Anna Stewart's stories have been published in *New Writing Dundee*, *Riptide Journal*, zine *Lives You Might Live*, and *Gutter*.

Shane Strachan's work has appeared in *New Writing Scotland*, *Northwords Now*, *Causeway/Cabhsair*, Freight's *Out There* anthology and many other publications.

Samuel Tongue has published poems in *Northwords Now*, *Magma*, *Gutter*, *The List*, *The Herald*, *Ink*, *Sweat and Tears*, *Be The First to Like This* and *Cordite*. He received a New Writers Award (Callan Gordon) in 2013.

George T Watt screives aamaist exclusively in Scots. He haes been published in *Lallans*, *New Writing Scotland*, *Ileach* and *Gutter*. He wis featured on BBC Ulster's Kist o Wurds an haes trie pamphlets.
www.georgetwatt.scot

Hamish Whyte is an Edinburgh-based poet, editor and publisher. His latest collection is *Hannah, Are You Listening?* (HappenStance).

Colin Will has had eight poetry books published. He chairs StAnza's Board, runs Calder Wood Press and The Open Mouse.

Olga Wojtas, half-Scottish and half-Polish, stays in Edinburgh and has just won a Scottish Book Trust New Writers Award.

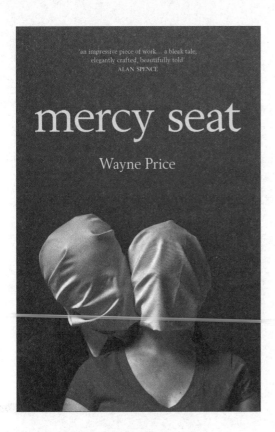

'an impressive piece of work... a bleak tale,
elegantly crafted, beautifully told'
ALAN SPENCE

mercy seat

Wayne Price

MERCY SEAT
Wayne Price

'Wayne Price is a fine poet and an accomplished short story writer, so
it's no surprise that his first novel, Mercy Seat, is an impressive piece of
work. In his characteristic spare, pared-down prose – not one word is
wasted – he tells a stark story of love and loss in harsh, troubled times.
It's a bleak tale, elegantly crafted, beautifully told (the handling of time
is masterly) and the telling itself becomes redemptive.'

ALAN SPENCE,

Author of *The Night Boat*,
The Pure Land and *Way to Go.*

**FREIGHT
BOOKS**

freightbooks.co.uk

RRP £8.99
Released: 23rd February
ISBN: 978-1-908754-98-1

IN THE EMPTY PLACES

• Short Stories and Art •

- - - - - - - - - - - - - - - - - - - -

An exciting and diverse collection by award-winning writers and artists from around the world, some translated into English for the first time. Available as an ebook (€5) or paperback (€15).

Featuring new work from Toni Davidson, Rodge Glass, Rodrigo Hasbún, Tendai Huchu, Kirsty Logan, Anneliese Mackintosh, Iain Maloney, Monica Metsers, Suhayl Saadi, Simon Sylvester, and Chiew-Siah Tei plus many more.

The Bantuan Coffee Foundation provides safe houses and education scholarships for the victims of child prostitution in Indonesia.
www.bantuancoffee.org

•